"*The Red Letter Life* reveals the changing power of Jesus' words read—and live!"

—Josh McDowell, internationally known author, lecturer, and Christian apologist

"Bob Hostetler is one of my favorite writers. I read everything he writes."

—Leonard Sweet, best-selling author, E. Stanley Jones Professor of Evangelism at Drew Theological School at Drew University and a Visiting Distinguished Professor at George Fox University

"Bob Hostetler. . .quotes the words of Jesus, astutely guiding us through familiar New Testament passages with fresh eyes, helping us see more clearly what Jesus expects his followers to do with their lives. The seventeen chosen words—'come,' 'follow,' and 'hear' among them—both challenge and convict us, comfort and encourage us. *The Red Letter Life* is a heartfelt invitation to put into action what Jesus put into words."

—Liz Curtis Higgs, best-selling author of *Bad Girls of the Bible: And What We Can Learn from Them*

"The Scriptures tell us the Word of God is alive and active. In *The Red Letter Life*, Bob Hostetler demonstrates how this is true. By asking us to hear some familiar words of Jesus with fresh ears, Bob shows the richness, depth, and transformative nature of Jesus' invitation and teaching. I highly recommend it!"

—Mike Erre, Senior Pastor of the First Evangelical Free Church of Fullerton, CA, and author of *Why the Bible Matters*

The RED
LETTER
Life

17 Words from **Jesus** to Inspire Simple, Practical, Purposeful Living

BOB HOSTETLER

SHILOH RUN  PRESS

An Imprint of Barbour Publishing, Inc.

Dedicated to my brothers,

Don and Larry

Print ISBN 978-1-62416-761-4

eBook Editions:
Adobe Digital Edition (.epub) 978-1-63058-101-5
Kindle and MobiPocket Edition (.prc) 978-1-63058-102-2

Published by Shiloh Run Press, an imprint of Barbour Publishing, Inc., P.O. Box 719, Uhrichsville, Ohio 44683, www.shilohrunpress.com

Our mission is to publish and distribute inspirational products offering exceptional value and biblical encouragement to the masses.

Member of the
Evangelical Christian
Publishers Association

Printed in the United States of America.

Acknowledgments

Thank you to my agent and friend, Steve Laube of the Steve Laube Agency, for representing me on this project.

Thank you to Kelly McIntosh, Dan Balow, and all the folks at Barbour Publishing, for seeing the value in this book and its message, and for the care, insight, and expertise that made it better at every point in the process.

Thank you to Dr. Ed Yamauchi for his expert counsel and advice. . .again.

Thank you to my prayer partners, who repeatedly supported me and this project in prayer: Bill Riley, Dewey Hughes, Tim Sheehan, and Doug Webb. Your ministry to me and to the readers of this book is deeply appreciated.

Thank you also—as always—to the lovely Robin, my wife, best friend, boon companion, confidante, lover, teacher, conscience, supporter, encourager, and muse.

Contents

THE FIRST WORD

I am a magazine junkie.

There. Now you know. It started long before I was a magazine editor, way back in the late 1980s. It goes back to my boyhood, sometime close to the dawn of civilization, when *Highlights* magazine came every month, when *The Weekly Reader* was better than an imaginary friend, and when a neighbor's copy of *Boy's Life* was worth my best marbles or baseball cards.

I haven't grown out of it yet. Even in this age of new digital media, I am irresistibly, inexorably drawn to good, old-fashioned print magazines. I could spend hours—and sometimes do—browsing the amazing array of shelved, shiny periodicals at my local books-and-coffee superstore. Or the several dozen titles available at the library. Or even the row upon row of publications available at the local grocery store.

One of my favorite magazines—besides *Men's Journal*, *Men's Health*, and *Manly Man Monthly*, of course—is a thick, slick monthly called *RealSimple*. It's a self-proclaimed "magazine about simplifying your life." It's kinda *Martha Stewart Living* for the nominally sane. But only nominally.

In *RealSimple*, you can get great ideas like dusting a lampshade with a lint roller; eight ways to use a can of beans; twenty-seven tips for wrapping, storing, and thawing all the foods you freeze; and how to make your own sandpaper with old grocery bags and kitty litter. (I might have made that last one up.)

I'm drawn to *RealSimple* not only because I appreciate a beautifully designed and produced magazine, but also because I admire the magazine's philosophy and approach, as identified in the tagline that graces every cover: "Life Made Easier."

LIFE MADE EASIER, EVERY DAY

You must admit, that's a fantastic line.

Who doesn't want life made easier? Whether it's "Twenty-Two Things You Didn't Know Your Dishwasher Could Do" or "Ten Easy Salad Recipes," I am constantly on the lookout for ways to make life easier.

Is it just me? Or do you also crave an easier life?

Several years ago I prompted nearly uncontrollable laughter from a landscape designer when I told her that my primary goal for my home and yard was not beauty, let alone elegance. "I'm going for maintenance-free," I said.

Oh, the hilarity that ensued. But I was serious. I know a completely maintenance-free home and yard may not be possible (I haven't achieved it yet, that's for sure), but I thought it was a worthwhile goal. I wanted "life made easier" every day.

That's sort of the idea of this book. But few people would ever associate such a concept with following Jesus or living a Christian life. They think quite different things when they hear the word *Christian* or *Christianity*.

To some people, it's all about loving your neighbor and just living a generally good life.

To others, it's about being white and Western and not Jewish. You know, if you're not Hindu and you're not Buddhist and you're not Muslim and you're not Jewish, well, then, you must be Christian.

For some, it's all about going to church, or keeping the Ten Commandments—or at least hanging them on your wall or posting them in your yard.

But those things are *not* Christianity—not even the "going to church" part. (That's why I wrote a book called *Quit Going to Church*. If you haven't read it yet, you should. You should even buy extra copies to give as gifts. In fact, if you want to go online or to the bookstore right now to do that, I won't mind. I'll wait right here until you get back.)

Christianity, when it's all said and done, is about following Jesus Christ and becoming every day more and more like him. That's where we got the word *Christian*. It was first used to describe people who were like Jesus, people who did what he said to do and resembled him in their attitudes and actions. They were not Christian as the word is often used today—someone who attends church or listens to "Christian music," who identifies with certain political causes or opposes various other causes. When the word was first coined, it referred to someone who *followed* Jesus.

But what did it mean to follow Jesus back then? And what does it mean today?

COME AND SEE

At the beginning of the Gospel of John, the last Gospel to be written (probably toward the end of the first century AD), the apostle John relates an incident that happened at the outset of Jesus' public ministry. Referring to John the Baptist, who has just announced to everybody who would listen that his cousin, Jesus of Nazareth, is the Lamb of God, the Preexistent One, who would baptize with fire, John the apostle writes this:

> *The next day John was there again with two of his disciples. When he saw Jesus passing by, he said, "Look, the Lamb of God!"*
>
> *When the two disciples heard him say this, they followed Jesus. Turning around, Jesus saw them following and asked, "What do you want?"*
>
> *They said, "Rabbi" (which means "Teacher"), "where are you staying?"*

"Come," he replied, "and you will see."

So they went and saw where he was staying, and they spent that day with him. It was about four in the afternoon.

Andrew, Simon Peter's brother, was one of the two who heard what John had said and who had followed Jesus. The first thing Andrew did was to find his brother Simon and tell him, "We have found the Messiah" (that is, the Christ). And he brought him to Jesus.

Jesus looked at him and said, "You are Simon son of John. You will be called Cephas" (which, when translated, is Peter).

The next day Jesus decided to leave for Galilee. Finding Philip, he said to him, "Follow me."

Philip, like Andrew and Peter, was from the town of Bethsaida. Philip found Nathanael and told him, "We have found the one Moses wrote about in the Law, and about whom the prophets also wrote—Jesus of Nazareth, the son of Joseph."

"Nazareth! Can anything good come from there?" Nathanael asked.

"Come and see," said Philip.[1]

John the Baptist was hanging out with two of his followers. We find out that one of them was Andrew of Bethsaida. The other was, quite possibly, the apostle John himself, the one who recorded this story. When John the Baptist sees Jesus and tells his companions, "Fellas, I'm tellin' ya, that's the Lamb of God," Andrew and John fall in step with Jesus. When Jesus notices them, he says, "What do you want?"

Other versions translate his question, "What do you seek?"[2] and "What are you looking for?"[3] It wasn't a simple "Whaddya want?" or "What can I do for you?" It was, rather, "What are you searching for?"

And the two men, in what are recorded as their first words to the Lamb of God, instead of saying, "We seek the Christ, the son of the Living God," or "We seek the Bread of Life," or even, "We seek answers," "We seek hope," "We seek deliverance," or "We seek eternal life," merely respond, "Where are you staying?"

Say *what*? "Where are you *staying*?" These two had been followers of John the Baptist. They had listened to his preaching. They had heard him refer to one who would come to take away the sin of the world. And they had just heard John identify Jesus with the words, "Look, the Lamb of God." But when they begin to follow this Lamb of God away from the scene and he asks what they are seeking, their answer is, "Where are you staying?" Are you serious?

Matthew Henry suggests that their question was simply to indicate their desire to become better acquainted with Jesus. That may be true, but I think their question indicates something else: *awkwardness.* They may have stuttered the answer, something like, "Um, uh, well, Rabbi, um, where are you staying?"

They may have been like many people today, who are drawn to Jesus and start heading his direction without really knowing what to expect. But they see something. They sense something. And they want more, even if they find it hard to express what it is they are seeking.

To such people, Jesus says the same thing he said to Andrew and his companion: "Come, and you will see."[4]

That is Jesus' first word to many human souls: "Come. Come and see."

Years ago, I was a pastor in a church in southwest Ohio. The leaders of that church had prayed, planned, and prepared for a series of candid Sunday messages entitled "God on Trial." The three weeks of that series tackled the reliability of the Bible, the identity of Jesus, and the validity of the Christian faith. A few weeks in advance, I stopped at the local print shop to pick up an array of promotional materials that had been ordered. The young woman who took my payment wrinkled her nose at the materials. I asked her if she would be interested in attending.

"Oh no," she said. "I think it's wrong."

She surprised me. I asked her what she objected to.

"I just think it's wrong, that's all."

I probed a little more and eventually learned that she was a churchgoer herself, but she objected to the idea of placing God "on trial." Her view, as well as I could extract it from her, was that God is not to be questioned, simply believed and accepted.

She was not interested in discussing matters further, so I thanked her sincerely and left the store. But I think I could see where she was coming from; she thought that investigating God and weighing his claims was an insult to his dignity and majesty.

But our God is a God who invites scrutiny. He says, "Come now, and let us reason together."[5] He says, "Taste and see that the LORD is good!"[6] He says, "Put me to the test."[7]

And now, in Christ, God says, "Come and see." Check it out. Look. Listen. Learn. Jesus invites us to inquire into him. He welcomes our questions. He will receive us, even with our doubts and faults. He says, "Whoever comes to me I will never drive away."[8]

COME AND REST

We human beings have an amazing capacity to complicate things.

When the first McDonald's restaurant opened, they offered burgers, fries, and beverages. When Henry Ford produced the first Model T, it had a twenty-horsepower engine, two forward gears, a single color (black), and no front doors. When Binney & Smith introduced the first Crayola crayons, there were eight colors in the box. These days, McDonald's offers 145 menu items; Ford offers an array of cars with numerous options, such as remote start and a rear-obstacle detection system; and Crayola packs as many as 120 colors and shades into a box of crayons.

Those are all improvements, right? But it can get overwhelming. It can become exhausting. Especially because that tendency to complicate things extends to our spiritual lives as well. Most of us, if we feel dissatisfied with our spiritual lives, will usually see it as a function of not doing enough. We will say things like, "I know what I need to do. I just need to read the Bible more." Or "I haven't been going to church like I should." Or "I just need to pray more." It's all about performance. Checklists. Rituals.

But that idea does not come from Jesus. He said:

> *"Come to me, all you who are weary and burdened, and I will give you rest. Take my yoke upon you and learn from me, for I am gentle and humble in heart, and you will find rest for your souls. For my yoke is easy and my burden is light."*[9]

When Jesus called people to himself, when he took a life and aligned it with his, his approach was invitational. It was highly personal. It was tailored to that person's need. And it was a relief, especially compared to the way of the Pharisees, who were constantly adding "thou shalts" and "thou shalt nots" to people's lives.

When you think of your spiritual life, do you think, *My burden is light?* Or do you think, *I'm not doing enough?* Maybe you hear a voice—a parent's or a pastor's or somebody else's—telling you that what you are doing is not enough. So you increase your efforts. You try harder. You get up earlier. You add to your already heavy daily load, in hopes of finding fulfillment and satisfaction. But Jesus says, "Come to me, all you who are weary and burdened, and I will give you rest."[10] He didn't say, "You're not doing enough." He said, "Come. . .and rest."

In Jesus' day, when a student decided to enroll in the school of a particular rabbi, he was said to take the rabbi's "yoke," a reference to the wooden beam used to connect a pair of oxen or other animals together so they can pull a wagon or plow in the same direction. It pictured the student walking the same way as the teacher, side by side, step by step. So when Jesus said, "My yoke is easy," he referred to the relative ease of going his way, side by side and step by step. He didn't claim to place *no* burden on his followers, but he did promise a *light* burden. If we come to Jesus and remain "heavy laden," then it is not his way we have taken. H

As a Christ-follower and as a pastor, I confess that too often I have been like the Pharisees, who, as Jesus said, "crush people with unbearable religious demands."[11] I have fallen into the performance trap. But the drive to perform leads to checklists—all the things I need to do to feel good about myself. Checklists lead to failure. Failure leads to shame. Shame leads to withdrawal. And withdrawal leads to emptiness.

Jesus says, "Come." He says, "Take my yoke." He says, "Walk with me. Go this way. Watch and learn. It's not about *doing*. . .it's about *being*. It's not about performance; it is about a person—*me*. Just be with me, and I will give you rest."

If you have not yet found forgiveness of sins and newness of life in Jesus Christ, I urge you to respond to his invitation, enter his rest, and experience release and relief from sin, guilt, checklists, failure, and more. You may start by saying something like this: "Jesus, I come to you, as you have invited me. Please forgive the wrong things I've done. Come into my heart and make it your home. And from this moment on, help me to take your yoke. To walk with you. To watch and learn. Help me to focus on being with you, rather than on trying to do all the right things. Thank you for your love and sacrifice, which makes this new life possible for me. Amen."

COME AND HEAL

Jesus is the fulfillment of the true seeker. He is the desire of the seeking heart. He is the healer of the wounded heart. And he says, simply, "Come."

You don't have to clean up your act.

You don't have to figure out everything first.

You don't have to understand everything.

You don't have to understand *anything*.

Just come.

The only prerequisite is "Come."

One Sabbath day, Jesus was teaching in the synagogue, nearly across the street from his friend Peter's house in Capernaum. A man with a deformed hand was there, and a group of Pharisees was watching carefully to see if Jesus would heal the man, so they could accuse him of breaking the Law by working on the Sabbath. Jesus was undeterred. He said to the man, "Come here."[12] Then he asked the crowd, "Is it lawful on the Sabbath to do good or to do harm, to save life or to kill?"[13] When no one answered, he told the man to stretch out his hand. Even as the man obeyed, his hand was healed, without a further word or action from Jesus.

The man's healing began with his response to the word, "Come." And so does yours.

Do you need healing from a long-ago wound? Your healing begins with your response to Jesus' invitation: "Come."

Are you holding on to resentment and bitterness toward someone who wronged you? Jesus says, "Come."

Do you wrestle with pain and affliction? Have you suffered a loss from which you think you can never recover? Are you suffering under a load that seems too heavy to bear? Your healing begins with your response to Jesus: "Come."

Your healing may not be complete at that point. Once, Jesus was in the village of Bethsaida, not far from the synagogue where he had healed the man with the withered hand. Some people presented a blind man to Jesus and begged him to heal the man. He took the man by the hand and led him out of the village, where he stopped, spit on the man's eyes, and rubbed them until the man could open them.

"Do you see anything?" Jesus asked.

"I see people," the man said. "They look like trees walking around."

At that, Jesus placed his hands on the man's eyes. When he removed his hands, the man's sight was completely restored. He saw everything clearly. He was healed.[14]

At the synagogue in Capernaum, Jesus simply spoke and the man's withered hand was healed. But in Bethsaida, he did things differently. He led the man out of the village. He spit on his eyes (maybe to soften the crusty secretions that kept the man's eyelids gummed together). He asked the man if he could see anything. Then he touched the man's eyes to complete the healing.

Why the differences? Why was one man healed without a touch, while the other apparently required a second touch? We don't know for sure, but it may serve to illustrate that healing sometimes comes in an instant and sometimes as the result of a process. Both are miraculous. Both are the work of God. One simply happens in stages, in multiple steps, for any number of reasons.

So go the next step with Jesus, and then trust him for the next step after that. And the one after that.

COME AND SUFFER

We are surrounded by hucksters and villains. We have become accustomed to salespeople and advertisers who will say and do anything to get our money. We are all too familiar with politicians and candidates who lie and cheat with alacrity. We feel like Charlie Brown, who has had the football snatched away at the last moment too many times, and we don't want to be suckered again.

You've probably never heard it put quite like this, but Jesus is a far cry from Charlie Brown's friend Lucy. He does not play fast and loose with the truth. In fact, truth is his very nature.[15] He once said:

> "*Suppose you want to build a tower. You would first sit down and figure out what it costs. Then you would see if you have enough money to finish it. Otherwise, if you lay a foundation and can't finish the building, everyone who watches will make fun of you. They'll say, 'This person started to build but couldn't finish the job.'*
>
> "*Or suppose a king is going to war against another king. He would first sit down and think things through. Can he and his 10,000 soldiers fight against a king with 20,000 soldiers? If he can't, he'll send ambassadors to ask for terms of peace while the other king is still far away.*"[16]

Makes sense, right? When you go to buy a house or a car, or sign up for a gym membership or time-share vacation, you want to know the bottom line: What does it cost? Jesus understands that. He actually endorses it. And he puts the price tag right up front:

> "*If people come to me and are not ready to abandon their fathers, mothers, wives, children, brothers, and sisters, as well as their own lives, they cannot be my disciples. So those who do not carry their crosses and follow me cannot be my disciples. . . . None of you can be my disciples unless you give up everything.*"[17]

Jesus of Nazareth is no huckster. He does not hide the price tag. He bids a man or woman, "Come and see," "Come and rest," "Come and heal." But there is more.

Dietrich Bonhoeffer was a pastor and theologian who lived in Germany prior to and during World War II. A man of integrity and conviction, he resisted the Nazi regime. Over time, he was forbidden to lecture, his seminary was shut down by the Nazis, and his writings were banned. In 1939 he traveled to New York at the invitation of Union Theological Seminary, and was strongly urged by friends to stay in America. He decided instead to return to Germany on the last scheduled steamer to cross the Atlantic. He was arrested by the Gestapo in 1943 and executed at the Flossenbürg concentration camp on April 9, 1945, just two weeks before American soldiers liberated the camp. Just a few years before, he had written these words:

> *When Christ calls a man, he bids him come and die. It may be a death like that of the first disciples who had to leave home and work to follow him, or it may be a death like Luther's, who had to leave the monastery and go out into the world. But it is the same death every time—death in Jesus Christ, the death of the old man at his call.* [18]

When Jesus says, "Come," it is an invitation unlike any other. It is an invitation to forgiveness and freedom. It is an invitation to healing and wholeness. It is an invitation to rest and release. But it is also an invitation to an execution—your own. That is the meaning of Jesus' words about carrying the cross.

To hear the claims of many authors and television preachers, Jesus will solve all your problems and make you happy, healthy, and wealthy. But Jesus didn't claim that. He never sugarcoated things. He promised abundant blessings but also referred to a life of following him as carrying a cross, something only convicted prisoners did as they walked to their death. As Bonhoeffer said, not everyone will face the martyrdom endured by the first disciples—and by

Bonhoeffer himself. Some, like Luther, will suffer differently. But all who come will suffer.

You will suffer temptation. Jesus himself was tempted, and he was the Son of God. Matthew, Mark, and Luke record some of his temptations (Matthew 4:1–11; Mark 1:12–13; Luke 4:1–13). He was tempted to take shortcuts. He was tempted to doubt his Father's timing. He was tempted to seek the approval of others. The Bible even says Jesus was "tempted in *every* way, just as we are."[19] But the person who responds to Jesus' invitation to "come" has a resource when tempted that others lack: "Because he himself suffered when he was tempted, he is able to help those who are being tempted."[20] He will not let you be tempted beyond what you can bear, and he will provide a way of escape.[21] This means you will never face a temptation you can't overcome, because the Lord is with you. He will help you.

You will suffer testing. Circumstances will arise in your life that will test the limits of your endurance. Of your patience. Of your faith. But the New Testament writer James says such tests ought to prompt joy rather than disappointment or discouragement:

> *Consider it pure joy, my brothers and sisters, whenever you*
> *face trials of many kinds, because you know that the testing*
> *of your faith produces perseverance. Let perseverance finish*
> *its work so that you may be mature and complete, not lacking*
> *anything.*[22]

As it is in school, so it is in life: only those who are preparing themselves for something better are subject to tests. Your tests are teaching you and preparing you for something more, something better, something beyond who you are and what you are capable of today.

You will suffer trouble. Jesus put it bluntly: "In this world you will have trouble."[23] He never said, "Come to me and your milk will never sour." He never promised, "Come to me and your business will succeed." He never claimed, "Come to me and your life will be one victory lap after another." He said, "In this world you will have trouble." But then he added, "Take heart! I have overcome the world."[24] Whatever affliction or calamity we may face in this world, it will not—cannot—be final, because "we are more than conquerors through him who loved us."[25]

You may suffer persecution. "That's my cross to bear," people say sometimes. They may be referring to their struggle with arthritis or diabetes. They may apply it to a wayward child or an aging parent. But none of those things, difficult as they are, qualify as the kind of cross Jesus said we must bear. When he said, "If any of you wants to be my follower, you must turn from your selfish ways, take up your cross daily, and follow me,"[26] he was referring to the kind of self-sacrifice demonstrated by John (who was exiled), Peter (who was crucified upside down), James (who was beheaded), and Paul (who was scourged, beaten with rods, stoned, imprisoned, and eventually executed). Even today, followers of Jesus are often imprisoned, tortured, and martyred because of their faith. You may not suffer such a fate, but you may nonetheless face persecution. Others may spread cruel rumors about you. You may be passed over for tenure or promotions. You may be vilified, even hounded, for peacefully and graciously expressing a Christian viewpoint. When that is the case, however, Jesus said it should prompt joy:

> *"Blessed are those who are persecuted because of righteousness, for theirs is the kingdom of heaven.*

> *"Blessed are you when people insult you, persecute you and falsely say all kinds of evil against you because of me. Rejoice and be glad, because great is your reward in heaven."*[27]

You will suffer attacks. People who respond to Jesus' call and draw close to God can expect spiritual attacks. A man named Job, who lived many centuries ago, had it made. . .until he became the central figure in a cosmic test. The first chapters of the book of Job tell how Satan unleashed merciless attacks on him *because* he was a faithful servant of God's.

Likewise with King Jehoshaphat. He was the son and successor of Asa, who had been king of Judah, the southern half of the nation that had once been ruled by King David and King Solomon. In Jehoshaphat's day, however, the nation was split in two, and Jehoshaphat fortified the southern kingdom against Israel, which was to the north, and against its notorious leader, King Ahab. Jehoshaphat also set out to do some mighty good things in God's eyes. He decided to rid the land of idolatry and return to the worship of the true God (1 Kings 22:43). He sent out priests over the land to instruct the people in the law (2 Chronicles 17:7–9), and as a result of his actions, he enjoyed a great measure of peace and prosperity, and the blessings of God rested on the people.

And that is when stuff started to go sour.

Which is how it often seems to work.

If you are not a rebuke or a threat to the influence of evil in this world, the devil may be content to leave you alone. But if you start responding to the voice of the Lord and fall into step with him, that is when you can expect the spiritual fur to fly, so to speak. That is when you will begin to experience attacks.

It's like the experience of a boy who was on my son Aaron's baseball team many years ago. (Aaron now has children of his own.) It was the first year after tee-ball, when coaches lobbed the ball to the batter. Despite the coach's best efforts to hit this one boy's bat with the ball, the little guy struck out. He ran to his father, crying, "He won't let me hit it, Daddy!" Although moved by his son's tears, the father didn't complain to the umpire or scream at the pitcher. He gripped his son's shoulders and faced him squarely. "He's not supposed to let you hit it, son," the man explained. "His job is to pitch the ball. Your job is to hit it. *That's baseball.*"

So it is. We should not be shocked when we experience spiritual attacks, *especially* when "things were going so well." It will happen. It is supposed to happen. Your enemy's "job," so to speak, is to prowl around "like a roaring lion looking for someone to devour."[28] Your job is to "resist him, standing firm in the faith."[29] And God's job? "After you have suffered a little while, [he] will himself restore you and make you strong, firm and steadfast."[30]

You can count on God to do his job. If you do yours, you need fear nothing from the enemy of your soul. He is a defeated foe. As one version of the hymn "A Mighty Fortress" puts it:

> *And though this world, with devils filled,*
> *Should threaten to undo us,*
> *We will not fear, for God hath willed*
> *His truth to triumph through us:*
> *The Prince of Darkness grim,*
> *We tremble not for him;*
> *His rage we can endure,*
> *For lo, his doom is sure;*
> *One little word shall fell him.*[31]

ONLY THE BEGINNING

Come.

What a simple word. One syllable. Four letters. Yet it can be the beginning of so much.

Have you heard Jesus saying, "Come"? Are you hearing it now? Again, perhaps?

If you haven't come to him to receive forgiveness of sins and new life, *come.*

If you've been edging him out of your life lately, forgetting him, neglecting him, ignoring him, *come.*

If you've been putting him off until you get a few things figured out or straightened around, just *come.*

If your heart is hurting, *come.*

If your soul feels like it is shrinking, *come.*

If your strength is depleted, *come.*

If you find it hard to even identify where you are or what you are feeling, *come.*

One little word. One small step. One tiny act of obedience. *Come.*

Whatever it looks like in your life, in your heart, in your need, at this point in your spiritual journey, right now, right here, *come.*

THE FINAL WORD

Each chapter in this book will conclude with a "final word," a short and practical way to respond to the content of the chapter you have just read. The first of these exercises, below, is one of the simplest.

The following lyric is the first verse of a hymn that has been sung for decades by millions around the world. Take a few moments to read aloud (or sing) the following lines. Make them your prayer and apply them to your current situation:

Out of my bondage, sorrow, and night,
Jesus, I come! Jesus, I come!
Into Thy freedom, gladness, and light,
Jesus, I come to Thee!
Out of my sickness into Thy health,
Out of my want and into Thy wealth,
Out of my sin and into Thyself,
Jesus, I come to Thee![32]

2

THE WORD FOR STARTING OVER

I use it on my computer. I need it in my life.

If you're anything like me, one of the most used functions on your computer is Ctrl-Z (or, in my case, since I use a Mac, Command-Z). It is the keyboard stroke for "undo."

Not long ago, I was in the process of printing multiple documents. After sending the files to my printer, I continued making changes in those documents. Then the printer jammed. It took some time to fix the misfeed and get the printer reset and ready to print again. But now the jammed documents needed to be reprinted.

First, I had to tell my computer to "undo" the changes I had made. Each time I pressed Command-Z, the latest change was undone. After I "undid" everything and printed out everything I wanted to print, I simply used another command—Command-Y—to restore all my changes and get back to where I had been when the printer rebelled.

If you use a computer with any regularity, you've probably done something similar. Command-Z has bailed me out of trouble more times than I care to admit.

Wouldn't it be nice if there were an "undo" command for life? A "reset" button? A rewind?

There sorta is.

THE MAN AT THE CROSSING

Imagine what it was like, two thousand years ago, to be a peasant Jew living in the land of your ancestors. Your freedoms are few. Your prospects are limited. Your family is poor, and your God seems distant. Having grown up under the oppression of a rude and arrogant occupying army, you have no reason to expect that your children will grow up differently.

But then you hear of a prophet who has appeared at "the crossing," a point in the Jordan River opposite Jericho, where your ancestors entered the land and began life anew—the place also where Elijah and Elisha parted the waters and introduced a new era in your people's history. The prophet's name is John—a common name—but people have started calling him "the Immerser," because he is telling people to wash in the river, like those who bathe in the *mikvah* before entering the temple to worship.

You decide to see for yourself. You pack a little food and a few coins in a bag and strike out. As you approach the spot, you hear a voice before you see anything; it rolls over the countryside in waves like thunder. You thread your way through the brush along the riverbank as you listen to the booming voice:

> *"A voice of one calling in the wilderness,*
> *'Prepare the way for the Lord,*
> *make straight paths for him.*
> *Every valley shall be filled in,*
> *every mountain and hill made low.*
> *The crooked roads shall become straight,*
> *the rough ways smooth.*
> *And all people will see God's salvation.'"* [33]

You break through the thick brush and join a circle of onlookers. You stand as tall as you can and finally manage to locate the speaker. He stands in the water, closer to the east bank. He is stripped to the waist, exposing a barrel chest covered with hair. He is not tall, but he stands in the water like something made of granite—solid, immovable, irresistible. He continues speaking.

"The Sovereign LORD is coming with power.
He will rule with a powerful arm.
See, he brings his reward with him as he comes.
He will feed his flock like a shepherd.
He will carry the lambs in his arms,
holding them close to his heart.
he will gently lead the mother sheep with their young."[34]

Even as he speaks, a stream of people wade out to him. One by one he receives them, like a priest. Placing a hand on each one's head, he pushes the person down, squatting into the water and holding for a moment before releasing the person.

You watch. You wait. And then you make your decision.

THE WORD FOR STARTING OVER

It is the word for starting over.

Repent.

It was the call that John the Immerser (or John the Baptist as he is more familiarly known) issued to the people of his region and generation. It was also the call of Jesus from the outset of his public ministry:

From that time Jesus began to preach, saying, "Repent, for the kingdom of heaven is at hand."[35]

John preached it, and Jesus commanded it. Repent. A simple, straightforward word.

It has a different ring in our ears, however, than it did to those who heard it from John's lips—and later from Jesus. Theologian N. T. Wright explains:

This is a classic example. . .of a phrase whose meaning has changed over the years. If I were to go out on the street in my local town and proclaim that people should "repent and believe," what they would hear would be a summons to give up their private sins (one suspects that in our culture sexual misbehavior and alcohol or drug abuse would come quickly to mind) and to "get religion" in some shape or form—either experiencing a new inner sense of God's presence, or believing a new body of dogma, or joining the church or some sub-branch of it. But that is by no means exactly what the phrase "repent and believe" meant in first-century Galilee.

How are we to unlearn our meanings for such a phrase and to hear it through first-century ears? It helps if we can find another author using it at around the same place and time as Jesus. Consider, for example, the Jewish aristocrat and historian Josephus, who was born a few years after Jesus' crucifixion and who was sent in AD 66 as a young army commander to sort out some rebel movements in Galilee. His task, as he describes it in his autobiography, was to persuade the hot-headed Galileans to stop their mad rush into revolt against Rome and to trust him and the other Jerusalem aristocrats to work out a better modus vivendi. So when he confronted the rebel leader, he says that he told him to give up his own agenda and to trust him, Josephus, instead. And the words he uses are remarkably familiar to readers of the Gospels: he told the brigand leader to "repent and believe in me," metanoēsein kai pistos emoi genesesthai.

This does not, of course, mean that Josephus was challenging the brigand leader (who, confusingly, was called "Jesus") to give up sinning and have a religious conversion experience. It has a far more specific and indeed political meaning. I suggest that when we examine Jesus of Nazareth forty years earlier going around Galilee telling people to

*repent and believe in him or in the Gospel, we dare not screen
out these meanings. Even if we end up suggesting that Jesus
meant more than Josephus did—that there were indeed
religious and theological dimensions to his invitation—we
cannot suppose that he meant less. He was telling his hearers
to give up their agendas and to trust him for his way of
being Israel, his way of bringing the kingdom, his kingdom-
agenda. In particular, he was urging them, as Josephus had,
to abandon their crazy dreams of nationalist revolution. But
whereas Josephus was opposed to armed revolution because he
was an aristocrat with a nest to feather, Jesus was opposed to
it because he saw it as, paradoxically, a way of being deeply
disloyal to Israel's God and to his purpose for Israel to be the
light of the world. And whereas Josephus was offering as a
counter agenda a way that they must have seen as compromise,
a shaky political solution cobbled together with sticky tape,
Jesus was offering as a counter-agenda an utterly risky way
of being Israel, the way of turning the other cheek and going
the second mile, the way of losing your life to gain it. This was
the kingdom-invitation he was issuing. This was the play for
which he was holding auditions.[36]*

To John, and to Jesus, the word *repent* did not mean "go forward
in a church service." It did not mean "say you're sorry for your sins."
It did not even mean "have a transformative religious experience."
The word itself—*teshuvah* in Hebrew—means "turn." In other
words, turn around. Stop going *this* way, and go *another* way instead.
We might call it "doing a 180."

That is why John's call to repentance involved a thorough
washing in the waters of the Jordan. It signified a complete cleansing
from the past—from old habits, old agendas, old priorities, stains,
and scars. And it meant a fresh start, a new direction, a "counter-
agenda" in the future. A *reset*. A Command-Z.

TURN FROM DARKNESS

When Matthew, one of Jesus' earliest biographers, set out to describe how Jesus started his public ministry, he related first how Jesus met John at the Jordan River to be immersed by him (not to wash away his past, because Jesus had committed no sin, but "to fulfill all righteousness").[37] Then he told how Jesus ventured into the harsh Judean desert to endure an intense period of privation and temptation—after which, Matthew says:

> *He went and lived in Capernaum, which was by the lake in the area of Zebulun and Naphtali—to fulfill what was said through the prophet Isaiah:*

> *"Land of Zebulun and land of Naphtali,*
> *the Way of the Sea, beyond the Jordan,*
> *Galilee of the Gentiles—*
> *the people living in darkness*
> *have seen a great light;*
> *on those living in the land of the shadow of death*
> *a light has dawned."*

> *From that time on Jesus began to preach, "Repent, for the kingdom of heaven has come near."[38]*

Matthew quoted Isaiah to show that Jesus' taking up residence in Capernaum, a thriving fishing town on the shore of the Sea of Galilee, was a fulfillment of prophecy about the coming of the Messiah. But he may have had even more in mind.

Notice that Isaiah refers to the Messiah's coming as a great light piercing the darkness. By quoting Isaiah's poetic pronouncement, Matthew contrasts Jesus' appearance in Galilee with darkness and shadow. In that context, then, he reports Jesus beginning to preach,

"Repent, for the kingdom of heaven has come near." In doing so, he depicts repentance—*teshuvah*—as a turning from darkness.

Whatever has darkened your life, your soul, your past, Jesus says: "Repent." "Turn." "Start again."

Is it the darkness of abuse? Have you been hurt? Victimized? Scared or scarred—emotionally, verbally, physically, sexually? Jesus says, "Turn from that darkness." Start again. Leave it behind. Adopt his agenda, and no one else's. Decide to accept what he says about you, not what someone else has said, in word or in deed. Choose to agree with Jesus and what his Word says about you.

Is yours the darkness of pornography? Perversion? Promiscuity? Jesus says, "*Teshuvah.*" "Turn. Start anew." "Have nothing to do with sexual immorality, impurity, lust, and evil desires."[39] Make a break with such things.

Is yours the darkness of pride? Greed? Selfish ambition? Jesus says, "Repent." Those things have no place in his kingdom, and his kingdom has come to you. Surrender your priorities and accept his kingdom agenda.

Is yours the darkness of hatred and anger? Bitterness? Resentment?

Is yours the darkness of addiction? Gluttony? Gossip?

Is yours the darkness of laziness? Ingratitude? Jealousy?

Jesus says, "Repent."

He announces that a new kingdom, the kingdom of heaven, is here. It is available. It is yours for the asking. For the choosing. For the turning.

TURN FROM DOUBT

Mark was another of Jesus' biographers. In fact, his account of Jesus' life and ministry was probably the first to be written and distributed after Jesus' death, resurrection, and ascension. Like Matthew, he begins his account of Jesus' ministry by mentioning

Jesus' being immersed by John and then heading into the Judean wilderness to be tempted for forty days and nights. Then he writes:

> *Jesus went into Galilee, proclaiming the good news of God. "The time has come," he said. "The kingdom of God has come near. Repent and believe the good news!"*[40]

Repent. . .and believe.

Turn from doubt.

Just as Josephus had urged the brigand leader to "repent and believe," Jesus tells us to turn away from doubt and believe something. Something new. Something different. Something important.

What is it that Jesus tells us to believe? "The good news." The announcement that Jesus has introduced a change. That he represents an alternative. That he makes possible another way. Eugene Peterson elaborates on this idea in his book *A Long Obedience in the Same Direction*:

> *Repentance is not an emotion. It is not feeling sorry for your sins. It is a decision. It is deciding that you have been wrong in supposing that you could manage your own life and be your own god; it is deciding that you were wrong in thinking that you had, or could get, the strength, education and training to make it on your own; it is deciding that you have been told a pack of lies about yourself and your neighbors and your world. And it is deciding that God in Jesus Christ is telling you the truth. Repentance is a realization that what God wants from you and what you want from God are not going to be achieved by doing the same old things, thinking the same old thoughts. Repentance is a decision to follow Jesus Christ and become his pilgrim in the path of peace.*[41]

In many people's minds, *repentance* has negative connotations. But Jesus says, "Repent and believe the *good* news!"[42] Turn from doubt; embrace belief. Turn from the bad, old ideas; adopt a new way of thinking and living. Turn from lies; grab hold of the truth. Turn from destructive, deadly patterns; pursue love and life!

Scot McKnight, in his book *The Jesus Creed*, writes:

> *Ever since Eve and Adam, we have been trying to hide from God, to no avail, for the Creator of Eden continues to summon us in our own gardens, asking, "Where are you?" Because we have learned to hide, we need new beginnings to set us free, and the new beginnings begin at our own Jordans when we tell the truth.* [43]

Jesus calls you to repent—to turn from doubt, to give up your old, unproductive ideas and ways, and to accept the new, fruitful ways of his kingdom. His call to repentance is a call to turn away from unbelief. To turn your back on the thought that you can manage your own life and be your own god. To reject any suspicion that you have, or can get, the strength, education, and training to make it on your own. To decide that God in Jesus Christ is telling you the truth about how life works. About how *your* life works. And to choose from this moment forward to live your life *his* way instead of your own.

It is, as Eugene Peterson writes, "a rejection that is also an acceptance, a leaving that develops into an arriving, a no to the world that is a yes to God." [44]

That is what Jesus meant when he said, "Repent and believe the *good news!*" [45]

That is repentance Jesus style.

That is turning from doubt.

That is *teshuvah*.

TURN FROM DEATH

Jesus' call to repentance is a call to turn from darkness and doubt. It is also a call to turn from *death*.

Luke, another of Jesus' first-century biographers, records a later instance when Jesus issued a call to repentance:

> *About this time Jesus was informed that Pilate had murdered some people from Galilee as they were offering sacrifices at the Temple. "Do you think those Galileans were worse sinners than all the other people from Galilee?" Jesus asked. "Is that why they suffered? Not at all! And you will perish, too, unless you repent of your sins and turn to God. And what about the eighteen people who died when the tower in Siloam fell on them? Were they the worst sinners in Jerusalem? No, and I tell you again that unless you repent, you will perish, too."* [46]

Historians and biblical scholars differ as to exactly what event Jesus refers to in these verses. It is possible that history (other than Luke's account) never recorded the incident. Whatever the details were, Jesus' response may suggest that someone was trying to induce him to express anti-Roman sentiments, perhaps to trap him. If so, Jesus didn't take the bait. Instead, he drew a parallel between the victims of political oppression and fatalities in a tragic accident to inform his listeners that no one should imagine that their own righteousness will save them from death and destruction. This is why he asked the rhetorical question, "Were they worse sinners than other people? Is that why they died?" The obvious answer is *no*, which underscores the fact that no one is "good enough" to escape death. The only remedy, then, according to Jesus, is to repent—to turn from death by giving up our darkness and doubt and signing up for the new life, the counter-agenda, the kingdom way of Jesus.

Jesus made it clear that turning from sin and turning to God is the way to go on living, whether we are "worse" sinners than anyone else or not. His point was not that repentance will guarantee us a life free from oppression or tragedy, but that repentance equals life. Turning from sin is turning from death. Turning to God is turning to life. It is the same message he gave to Nicodemus when he told him, "You must be born again."[47]

Repent.

It is the word for starting over.

It is the word for beginning again.

It is the word for "reset." For "undo." For choosing light over darkness. For trusting in Jesus in place of doubt. For choosing life in him instead of death.

It is, as Eugene Peterson describes it, "the most practical of all words and the most practical of all acts. It is a feet-on-the-ground kind of word."[48]

It is not an emotion. It can be the act of a moment, but it must also be an ongoing attitude. A daily choice. A moment-by-moment reality.

Change direction. Start over. Begin again.

Teshuvah. Turn. Repent.

THE FINAL WORD

Many years ago, I reached a turning point. I had previously lived for myself—my own agenda, my own desires, my own needs and wants. And then I met a lovely woman named Robin. Within a very short time, my attitude and agenda changed—to the extent that I asked her to marry me. She shocked me by saying yes, and then by following through on her promise by saying "I do" in front of many of our family and friends. I said "I do," too. And when I did, I turned a corner. I no longer lived for myself, for my own agenda, desires, needs, and wants.

That turning point in my life has had daily application ever since. I have continued on that path. I have progressed in that purpose. I have grown in my capacity to love my wife.

That journey parallels the path of repentance.

You may have repented of your sins long ago. You may have knelt at an altar or prayed with a pastor. You may have tearfully confessed your brokenness and sinfulness and experienced the forgiveness and cleansing that only Jesus Christ can give.

That was my experience. But the *teshuvah* to which Jesus calls us is not limited to such an experience. It can be—and should be—a ruling feature of our lives. It has daily application. It is not a onetime event but an ongoing attitude. A constant determination. A moment-by-moment reality.

So here is the final word on this topic. Earlier in the chapter, I quoted a paragraph from Eugene Peterson's book *A Long Obedience in the Same Direction*, in which he defines repentance. I'd like for you to hand-copy that excerpt—once on each side of an index card, using a different color ink on the other side (or printing on one side and writing in script on the other). Place the card on your bathroom counter or bedside table. Each morning, before leaving your bedroom, read those words aloud, and then turn the card over (as a physical way of enacting *teshuvah*) and put it back in its place. Repeat this exercise every morning (and evening, if you wish) for the next week. Ask God's Holy Spirit to reflect those words—and the spirit of *teshuvah*—in your attitudes and actions throughout the day.

THE WORD THAT
PRECEDES OTHER WORDS

Sometimes you just want to hear some good news.

We get enough bad news in the course of a day or a week. Our television and radio airwaves are filled with reports of crime and war and tragedy. Newspapers and magazines carry stories of divorce, disease, and death. The mail brings little besides junk and bills.

TV producer Geri Weis-Corbley was fed up with the constant barrage of bad news, so she started something called the Good News Network (www.goodnewsnetwork.org). She calls it a "clearinghouse for the gathering and dissemination of positive compelling news stories from all sources around the globe." [49] Since its 1997 debut, her site has published good news daily and attracted tens of thousands of subscribers by featuring stories such as "Pope Francis Invites Boy with Down Syndrome for Spin on Popemobile," "Thai Prime Minister Announces End to Ivory Trade," and "Woman Loses 276 Pounds with Simple Plan Instead of Surgery."

Though Weis-Corbley allows that it is not necessary or desirable to avoid all negative news, she says, "We are in dire need of a well-balanced media diet. Local TV news, especially, has been continually feeding us junk food. We need to be informed by a world view that is not dripping with sensationalism and attuned to the police scanner." [50] She believes that her positive news can measurably improve our lives by fostering emotional well-being, health, and even prosperity.

I think Jesus would like Geri Weis-Corbley and the Good News Network. After all, the news of his life, ministry, and message has been called the Good News for two millennia now. And one of the words he used most frequently was a call to hear good news.

It is something we all need from time to time. Maybe it is something you need today. Perhaps you have been battered and dragged down by a recent spate of bad news. You may feel bowed under the weight of misfortune and mistakes. Maybe you've begun to feel that you may never hear good news again.

If any of those things ring true—even partially—you need the word that precedes other words.

JESUS' FIRST PRAYER

We don't know much about Jesus' childhood and adolescence. The Bible records only one incident in his life between his infancy and the launch of his ministry when he was around thirty years old. Extrabiblical sources are either silent on that period of his life or clearly spurious.

But one thing we know about Jesus' upbringing. We know what he prayed.

He was born into a Jewish family. We know from the accounts of his birth and earliest days of life that his parents were observant Jews. They obeyed the Law of Moses. They worshipped at the temple. They raised Jesus according to the requirements of their faith. So we can be confident that *shema* was among the first words he learned.

The *Shema* was the first prayer and portion of scripture Jewish children learned; it still is. Jesus' parents would have taught him to pray the *Shema* at least twice a day, in the morning and in the evening. It dated back many centuries, to a time when Moses and his people were newly delivered from slavery in Egypt, and it became the daily affirmation of observant Jews. Its origins are described in the book of Deuteronomy. When Moses transmitted God's Law to the people at Mount Sinai, he said:

Hear, O Israel: The LORD our God, the LORD is one. Love the
LORD your God with all your heart and with all your soul and
with all your strength. These commandments that I give you
today are to be on your hearts. Impress them on your children.
Talk about them when you sit at home and when you walk
along the road, when you lie down and when you get up.
Tie them as symbols on your hands and bind them on your
foreheads. Write them on the doorframes of your houses and on
your gates. [51]

It is called the *Shema* because the first word—*hear*—is the
Hebrew word *shema*. It is the word that precedes the central tenet
of Judaism: "The LORD our God, the LORD is one" (or, in some
renderings, "The LORD is our God, the LORD alone"). It is the
word that precedes the great commandment: "Love the LORD your
God with all your heart and with all your soul and with all your
strength."[52] It is the word that precedes what author Scot McKnight
calls "a Torah lifestyle" of memorization, recitation, instruction, and
physical reinforcement.[53]

The *Shema* was central to Jesus' ministry and message. One day,
one of his opponents asked him a fundamental question: "Teacher,
which is the greatest commandment in the Law?" Jesus answered
with part of the *Shema*—" 'Love the Lord your God with all your
heart and with all your soul and with all your mind.' This is the
first and greatest commandment"—before adding a twist: "And the
second is like it: 'Love your neighbor as yourself.' All the Law and
the Prophets hang on these two commandments."[54]

His mention of the *Shema* would have been an expected answer.
It was by no means groundbreaking, except when Jesus amended
the great commandment to include loving one's neighbor.

But he went even further. Throughout his public ministry, he
repeatedly pronounced *shema* in a new way, with fresh emphasis.

We lose some of the impact of his words because we read them in English, but when he spoke them initially, he used Aramaic, a language similar to Hebrew. And in Aramaic, as in Hebrew, the word he used would have been *shema*: "Whoever has ears," he often said, "let them hear [*shema*]."[55]

SHEMA: SOMETHING GOOD HAS COME TO YOU

The Gospel of Matthew, the first of four biblical accounts of Jesus' life, relates what Jesus said sometime after his cousin John was imprisoned by King Herod:

> *Now when John heard in prison about the things Jesus was doing, he sent word by his disciples to Jesus, asking, "Are you the one who is to come, or should we look for another?"*
>
> *Jesus responded, "Go, report to John what you hear and see. Those who were blind are able to see. Those who were crippled are walking. People with skin diseases are cleansed. Those who were deaf now hear. Those who were dead are raised up. The poor have good news proclaimed to them. Happy are those who don't stumble and fall because of me."*
>
> *When John's disciples had gone, Jesus spoke to the crowds about John: "What did you go out to the wilderness to see? A stalk blowing in the wind? What did you go out to see? A man dressed up in refined clothes? Look, those who wear refined clothes are in royal palaces. What did you go out to see? A prophet? Yes, I tell you, and more than a prophet. He is the one of whom it is written: Look, I'm sending my messenger before you, who will prepare your way before you.*
>
> *"I assure you that no one who has ever been born is greater than John the Baptist. Yet whoever is least in the kingdom of heaven is greater than he. From the days of John the Baptist until now the kingdom of heaven is violently attacked*

as violent people seize it. All the Prophets and the Law
prophesied until John came. If you are willing to accept it, he is
Elijah who is to come. Let the person who has ears, hear." [56]

John had been Jesus' "opening act," so to speak. He had
introduced Jesus as the Messiah, the Christ, the Lamb of God who
had come into the world to set things right. But, like most other Jews
of his day, John more or less expected Jesus to overthrow Rome and
establish a righteous kingdom, God's kingdom. He certainly didn't
expect, once Jesus arrived on the stage, to be arrested, imprisoned,
and in fear of his life. So when those things happened, John sent
messengers to ask Jesus, "What's going on?"

Jesus answered, "Tell John everything is on course. I am
fulfilling my mission. I am ushering in the kingdom: the blind are
receiving sight, the lame are walking, lepers are clean, deaf people
can hear. The dead are being brought back to life, and the poor are
hearing the news of the change I am introducing!"

Then, to the crowd that surrounded him, he went on to clarify
that John was, indeed, the forerunner, the "Elijah" the prophet
Malachi had said would announce the Messiah's coming.[57] Jesus
wanted people to know that the kingdom of God had truly arrived—
though its coming did not conform to all their expectations.
Theologian N. T. Wright writes:

> *Throughout his brief public career Jesus spoke and acted as if*
> *God's plan of salvation and justice for Israel and the world*
> *was being unveiled through his own presence, his own work,*
> *his own fate.. . .*
>
> *He told stories whose many dimensions cracked open the*
> *worldview of his hearers and forced them to come to terms*
> *with God's reality breaking in to their midst, doing what*
> *they had always longed for but doing it in ways that were so*
> *startling as to be hardly recognizable.* [58]

That's why Jesus said, "Whoever has ears, *shema.*" He knew not everyone would recognize the new reality he was ushering in. He knew that many, like John, would question it. Some would miss it entirely. But that didn't make it any less real or any less powerful.

Jesus says as much to you and me today. Whoever we are, wherever we are, he says, "Hear this: Something good has come to you. The kingdom is here. Healing is here. Blessing is here. Don't miss it." He comes to us today as he came long ago to the world. He comes to open our eyes. He comes to heal our hearts. He comes to make things right inside us and through us and all around us.

Whoever has ears, *shema.*

SHEMA: GET READY TO RECEIVE

Three times (out of seven) when the Bible records Jesus using the phrase "Whoever has ears, *shema,*" it follows the same story, which is told in Matthew, Mark, and Luke:

> *When a great crowd was gathering and people from town after town came to him, [Jesus] said in a parable: "A sower went out to sow his seed. And as he sowed, some fell along the path and was trampled underfoot, and the birds of the air devoured it. And some fell on the rock, and as it grew up, it withered away, because it had no moisture. And some fell among thorns, and the thorns grew up with it and choked it. And some fell into good soil and grew and yielded a hundredfold." As he said these things, he called out, "He who has ears to hear, let him hear."* [59]

It is one of Jesus' most familiar parables. If he had been a recording artist, it would have been on his Greatest Hits album. He explained to his closest friends and followers that the seed in his story represented the Word of God, which not everyone receives in the same way. Some people are like the soil along a well-traveled path, and the message never finds purchase in their hearts and is quickly snatched away by their enemy, the devil. Some are like the rocky soil; though they recognize and accept what God says, it never gets rooted enough to withstand storms and heat. Still others are like the soil in a bramble patch; the seed may take root, but it is eventually choked to death by other things—money, pleasure, etc. But some people are like "the good soil" in Jesus' story, who receive God's words and treasure them and nurture them until they produce a bountiful harvest.

Francis Chan, in his book *Crazy Love*, writes:

> *My caution to you is this: Do not assume you are good soil. I think most American churchgoers are the soil that chokes the seed because of all the thorns. Thorns are anything that distracts us from God. When we want God and a bunch of other stuff, then that means we have thorns in our soil. A relationship with God simply cannot grow when money, sins, activities, favorite sports teams, addictions, or commitments are piled on top of it.*
>
> *Most of us have too much in our lives. As David Goetz writes, "Too much of the good life ends up being toxic, deforming us spiritually." A lot of things are good by themselves, but all of it together keeps us from living healthy, fruitful lives for God.*
>
> *I will say it again: Do not assume you are good soil. Has your relationship with God actually changed the way you live? Do you see evidence of God's kingdom in your life? Are you choking it out slowly by spending too much time, energy, money, and thought on the things of this world?* [60]

Jesus says, "*Shema*: get ready to receive." The words of God are coming to you clearly and constantly. They come to you in the pages of your Bible, which is not merely the record of God's long-ago words to a long-ago people; it is also his thoroughly real and current word to you. The words of God come to you through the people who cross your path, the godly men and women who can help you listen, the pastors and prophets God has placed in your life—even the books he sometimes puts in your hands. The words of God come to you also in the quiet. In the night. In the dark. In those moments when the noise and the traffic slow and stop, and you become still enough to hear his voice. And his words also sometimes come through pain; through some injury or infirmity that brings you up short and may even leave you with a limp, like Jacob at Peniel,[61] but also tells you something you could not have heard otherwise.

So get ready to hear; get ready to receive. Soften the soil of your heart. Find ways to get on God's wavelength. Position yourself to pick up his signals. Read your Bible. Slow yourself down. Get quiet. Adjust your priorities. Figure out what it will take for *you* to receive God's words and treasure them and nurture them until they produce a bountiful harvest.

Whoever has ears, *shema*.

SHEMA: YOU ARE IN A STRUGGLE

Another story Jesus told is similar to the parable of the soils, and it was another occasion when he used the phrase "If you have ears to hear, *shema*."

> *He put another parable before them, saying, "The kingdom of heaven may be compared to a man who sowed good seed in his field, but while his men were sleeping, his enemy came and sowed weeds among the wheat and went away. So when the plants came up and bore grain, then the weeds appeared also.*

And the servants of the master of the house came and said to him, 'Master, did you not sow good seed in your field? How then does it have weeds?' He said to them, 'An enemy has done this.' So the servants said to him, 'Then do you want us to go and gather them?' But he said, 'No, lest in gathering the weeds you root up the wheat along with them. Let both grow together until the harvest, and at harvest time I will tell the reapers, Gather the weeds first and bind them in bundles to be burned, but gather the wheat into my barn.' ". . .

Then he left the crowds and went into the house. And his disciples came to him, saying, "Explain to us the parable of the weeds of the field." He answered, "The one who sows the good seed is the Son of Man. The field is the world, and the good seed is the sons of the kingdom. The weeds are the sons of the evil one, and the enemy who sowed them is the devil. The harvest is the end of the age, and the reapers are angels. Just as the weeds are gathered and burned with fire, so will it be at the end of the age. The Son of Man will send his angels, and they will gather out of his kingdom all causes of sin and all law-breakers, and throw them into the fiery furnace. In that place there will be weeping and gnashing of teeth. Then the righteous will shine like the sun in the kingdom of their Father. He who has ears, let him hear."[62]

Whole books have been written on this passage, but we will have to be satisfied with a few key points. Jesus urges his closest friends and followers to hear, to listen closely, to the parable, because it holds some important truths. And these truths are just as critical and relevant for us today:

You have an enemy. Jesus makes this point in the parable of the soils, too, when he explains that the soil along the path represents "the ones who hear, and then the devil comes and takes away the word from their hearts, so that they may not believe and be saved."[63] Similarly, in the parable of the wheat, Jesus explains that our enemy, the devil, sows weeds among the wheat. In other words, wherever we go and whatever we do, there will be people our enemy uses to hurt us, oppose us, choke off our effectiveness, and generally make our lives and our witness harder than they should be. It would be nice if it weren't so, but Jesus himself says that it is. . .and that it will continue to be so until the end of the age.

You will experience attacks. Notice that Jesus said, "When the plants came up and bore grain, then the weeds appeared also."[64] When you start bearing fruit—when you start getting serious about the things of God; when you start moving forward in faith; when you put forth prayerful, trusting efforts to do what God is calling you to do; when you start making a difference and changing the spiritual landscape, so to speak—that's when you can expect the weeds to appear. It should not surprise you. It should not derail you. In fact, you should learn to expect it. Not everything is a spiritual attack, of course. Not every negative person or circumstance is under the devil's control. But if you are advancing and making progress, you should not be surprised if you draw enemy fire.

You can be grateful that the harvest is delayed. In Jesus' parable, he depicts the farmer's servants asking if they should uproot the weeds. (After all, we all want God to put things right—*right now!*) But the farmer answers, "No, lest in gathering the weeds you root up the wheat along with them."[65] In other words, his delay is merciful. As Peter writes to suffering Christ-followers, "The Lord is not slow to fulfill his promise as some count slowness, but is patient toward you, not wishing that any should perish, but that all should reach repentance."[66] It can be hard to endure the slings and arrows of our enemy's attacks, but our Lord is not being slow; he is being patient; because some of us are still growing and learning, and many are not yet ready to be gathered.

Whoever has ears, *shema*.

SHEMA: YOU HAVE A PURPOSE

The Gospels of Mark and Luke record two more times when Jesus used the expression, "If anyone has ears to hear, let him hear":

> *And he said to them, "Is a lamp brought in to be put under a basket, or under a bed, and not on a stand? For nothing is hidden except to be made manifest; nor is anything secret except to come to light. If anyone has ears to hear, let him hear."* [67]

> *"Salt is good, but if salt has lost its taste, how shall its saltiness be restored? It is of no use either for the soil or for the manure pile. It is thrown away. He who has ears to hear, let him hear."* [68]

In each case, Jesus tells his listeners, "*Shema,*" to drive home the point that they have a purpose. A mission. A raison d'être. And so do you.

You are light, Jesus said. As Paul the apostle puts it, "At one time you were darkness, but now you are light in the Lord. Walk as children of light." [69] You don't need to search anxiously for your purpose in life; your purpose is to dispel darkness and shed light wherever you go.

Jesus said you are salt. Salt served two primary functions in the ancient world: it was a preservative and a seasoning. Similarly, if you are a follower of Jesus, you must, by your conduct and testimony, do your part to keep this world (or your corner of it) from becoming worse than it already is, and also add beauty, flavor—and even spice—to every situation and relationship you touch.

Whoever has ears, *shema.*

THE FINAL WORD

When Jesus says, "*Shema*," we should listen. In each of the seven instances in the Gospels when Jesus says, "*Shema*," he seems to intend for people to understand that something great is coming to them, they should be ready to receive what God says to them, and they should recognize the struggle they are in and embrace the purpose to which they were called.

I believe something great is coming to you. . .but you must be ready to receive it. It may well involve a struggle (present or future), and it may point you toward your purpose. So the final word for this chapter is *shema*. Hear. Listen.

I want to suggest that you make one change in your daily routine that will make space for you to hear from God. You may be in the habit of listening to the radio on your daily commute; what if you turned off the radio for five or ten minutes and asked God to speak to you? Or you may read the morning paper at the breakfast table; what if you sipped your last cup of coffee in silent meditation instead? Or what if you parked a little farther away from the grocery store doors and used the additional walking distance to listen for God's voice in the midst of your hectic schedule?

Maybe none of these suggestions work for you. But something will. Just one small change. What is it? Ask God. Make this moment right now a *listening* moment as you ask God to suggest something to you.

Whoever has ears, *shema*.

THE WORD THAT INVITES

I discovered early in life that I had a knack for drawing.

Maybe it was because people encouraged me. Or maybe people encouraged me because I didn't seem to have anything else going for me. Either way, I spent hours as a child sketching all sorts of things: cars, horses, dogs, people, cartoon figures, and more.

It wasn't long before I discovered that it was much easier to copy something than to sketch from memory—or invent something out of thin air, so to speak. I could pretty accurately duplicate someone else's sketch or painting. I could approximate a photograph. I could draw a still life or scene from real life. But it was a much greater challenge to sketch something from scratch.

It's the same for me in other areas of life, too. I can lose weight if you give me a program to follow, but don't expect me just to "eat responsibly." I do best when I'm given a guide or pattern to follow. I like "six steps to success" or "square-foot gardening." I like "do this" and "don't do that."

I think most of us are like that. We work better when we are given a model or pattern to follow. It's why God gave his people the Ten Commandments. It's why Jesus (when pressed) gave his followers the Lord's Prayer. And it's why Jesus said to Peter, James, and John (among others), "Follow me." He issues the same call to you and me today.

A SIMPLE CALL
Somewhere along the line, many churches and churchgoing folk have come to think about Jesus and the way of salvation in ways that don't necessarily jibe with what he said and did. For example,

many people equate "going to church" with "being a Christian." But Jesus' earliest followers never spoke or wrote in those terms. There was no such thing as "going to church" in those early days. The first generation to be called Christians worshipped together on Sundays, but their focus wasn't on "going to church," per se, but on learning from the apostles, spending time in one another's homes, sharing meals together, and praying together.[70]

Other "church folk" tend to think of "coming to Jesus" as basically praying a prayer and asking Jesus into your heart. To be fair, that is how many of us began our journey with Jesus. I knelt at a children's church altar and repeated a prayer, phrase by phrase, after the longsuffering Mrs. Reed. Many thousands trace the beginning of their faith journey to a moment when they prayed "the sinner's prayer," perhaps in a form suggested by evangelists such as Billy Graham or Bill Bright (author of *The Four Spiritual Laws* pamphlets). But Jesus himself never urged anyone to pray "the sinner's prayer." His preferred terminology was not "asking Jesus into your heart."

His call was—and is—simply, "Follow me." To a fisherman, he presented the call to follow as a call to join him in fishing. . .for men and women. To a Pharisee, he suggested that a life of following him would be like being born all over again. To a Samaritan woman, he depicted a life of following him as a long, refreshing drink of water. But though he used unique word pictures with different people, the call was always the same: *Follow.*

BREAK WITH YOUR PAST

The Gospel of Matthew is the first of four biographies of Jesus in the Bible. It is named after Matthew (who was also called Levi), one of Jesus' first twelve disciples, because he is credited as the author of the account. In the ninth chapter, Matthew records the following:

*When Jesus was leaving, he saw a man named Matthew
sitting in the tax collector's booth. Jesus said to him, "Follow
me," and he stood up and followed Jesus.* [71]

A lot is going on in that verse, not all of which is obvious to people reading those words in the twenty-first century. First, we must understand that Jesus was Jewish. You knew that already, right? But it helps to be reminded, particularly because he was also a rabbi. You may also have known that. But the verse above (as well as many others) shows us Jesus, the Jewish rabbi, beginning to assemble a school of students or followers. And that's where it gets really interesting.

In Jesus' day, rabbis were more or less like our colleges and universities today. If you wanted to study with a certain rabbi, you applied for acceptance into his "school." If the rabbi considered you to be good enough—a promising student, someone who would bring credit to him and his school—he would accept you.

But notice: that is not what Jesus did. The Bible is clear on this point. Peter and Andrew, James and John, and so on, did not apply to Rabbi Jesus. They did not choose him; *he* chose *them*. So it was with Matthew. Jesus saw him "sitting in the tax collector's booth." [72] And he said, "Follow me."

The call of Jesus to Matthew was not to pray a short prayer and thereafter call himself a Christian. It is clear in Matthew 9:9 that Matthew understood that Jesus' call required a break with his past. In Matthew's case, as a tax collector, it meant no more tax collecting. It meant no more cheating taxpayers. It meant no longer threatening and oppressing people. It meant giving up a lucrative business, and perhaps even leaving behind all he had built and bought in his career as a taxman. But Matthew succinctly describes that decision: "He stood up and followed Jesus." [73] He broke with his past. He left it all behind.

But there was another side to Matthew's response as well. As a tax collector in that day and age, he never would have expected any rabbi to accept him as a *talmid*, a student or disciple. Tax collectors were despised. They were seen as collaborators with Rome. Traitors. The worst kind of sinners. The lowest of the low to religious Jews. No self-respecting rabbi would have even looked at an application from Matthew—even if he used his Jewish name, Levi—let alone taken the initiative and *called* such a man into his school. But Jesus did. And in so doing, he sent a message.

No one is too low to follow Jesus. No one is too damaged. No one is unqualified. If Jesus called Matthew, he will not be repelled or repulsed by you. But as with Matthew, so with you. Following Jesus will mean a break with your past. It doesn't mean you have to "have it all together." It doesn't mean you have to "clean up your act" before you can come to him. But it does mean turning, as we discussed in chapter 2. It does mean starting over. It may mean giving up whatever stands between you and your rabbi. It means leaving behind anything that would divide your loyalties and impede your obedience. It also means letting go of all the guilt and shame in your past—all the wounds, all the pain, all the fear. It means mindfully, immediately, and irrevocably taking a stand. . .and following Jesus.

REORDER YOUR PRIORITIES

Some of the people Jesus called to follow him didn't do so. One of those was a wealthy young man whom Jesus knew and loved. We don't know the man's name, but the Gospel writer Mark tells his story:

> *As [Jesus] was setting out on [a] journey, a man ran up and knelt before him and asked him, "Good Teacher, what must I do to inherit eternal life?" And Jesus said to him, "Why do you*

call me good? No one is good except God alone. You know the commandments: 'Do not murder, Do not commit adultery, Do not steal, Do not bear false witness, Do not defraud, Honor your father and mother.' " And he said to him, "Teacher, all these I have kept from my youth." And Jesus, looking at him, loved him, and said to him, "You lack one thing: go, sell all that you have and give to the poor, and you will have treasure in heaven; and come, follow me." Disheartened by the saying, he went away sorrowful, for he had great possessions.

And Jesus looked around and said to his disciples, "How difficult it will be for those who have wealth to enter the kingdom of God!" And the disciples were amazed at his words. But Jesus said to them again, "Children, how difficult it is to enter the kingdom of God! It is easier for a camel to go through the eye of a needle than for a rich person to enter the kingdom of God." And they were exceedingly astonished, and said to him, "Then who can be saved?" Jesus looked at them and said, "With man it is impossible, but not with God. For all things are possible with God." [74]

Interestingly, this is the only recorded instance of Jesus telling someone to sell his possessions before becoming his follower. He apparently didn't say it to Matthew. He didn't say it to Peter (who evidently still owned a fishing boat after three years of following Jesus)[75] or any of his other disciples. But he said it to this young man. Why?

I think the text gives us a hint. When Jesus told this young man that inheriting the kingdom of heaven was a "simple" matter of obeying God's commands, the man answered, "All these I have kept from my youth."[76] Notice: "*all* these." And that's when Mark says, "Jesus, looking at him, loved him."

I think Jesus' look of love was something like that of a mother who knows her child has tried to flush the cat down the toilet and yet insists, "I didn't do it." Because, of course, this fellow was claiming to have kept *all* the commandments from his youth, and Jesus knew better. So he challenged the man's adherence to the first commandment: "Love the LORD your God with all your heart and with all your soul and with all your might."[77] Surely, if the man had truly kept all the commandments from his youth to the present day, then his response would reveal God to be first in his life, rather than money—right?

Even more so, the invitation of Rabbi Jesus to join his school—"and come, follow me"—would have sealed the deal, don't you think? Anyone who was so righteous as to have kept all the commandments of God from his youth would have broken with his past, with his wealth, with any and all earthly entanglements, and become one of the Twelve.

But that is not how this man's story ends. It concludes, "Disheartened by the saying, he went away sorrowful, for he had great possessions."[78]

"He had great possessions," Mark said. He also could have written, "His great possessions had him." He had his priorities, and "treasure in heaven" was a lower priority than "treasure on earth." Being rich was more important to him than following Jesus. Jesus challenged him to reorder his priorities, and the man walked away, sorrowful.

A passage in Luke's Gospel (Luke 9:57–62) tells of three more unnamed people who might have become apostles, authored Gospels, and entered the Hall of Faith in Hebrews 11. One vowed to follow Jesus anywhere, but Jesus warned him against such an impulsive response: "Foxes have holes, and birds of the air have nests, but the Son of Man has nowhere to lay his head."[79] A man whom Jesus called to follow him asked for a delay to bury his father (most likely to wait up to a year before the father's bones would be reburied in an ossuary, a common practice in Jesus' day); Jesus urged the man to prioritize the kingdom of God over a funeral. And another man appealed to one of the strongest loyalties in Jewish society: family. "Yes Lord, I will follow you," he said, "but let me first say good-bye to my family." [80] Even that, Jesus refused, thus making it clear that even otherwise righteous priorities must take second place to following him.

The call of Jesus to follow him is a call to reorder your priorities. Don't kid yourself into thinking you have kept "all these" from your youth; if you can follow Jesus without reordering your priorities, then you have misunderstood and misdefined *following*. Accept no excuse, no equivocation, no delay. When Jesus says, "Follow me," he intends to be placed first in your heart, mind, soul, and life. Your wealth, your comfort, your convenience—even your family—must take a backseat. Because that is what Jesus means when he says, "Follow me."

GO WHERE JESUS GOES

You may recall Jesus' response to a couple of his cousin John's disciples. We discussed it in chapter 1, but it bears another look here:

> *The next day John was there again with two of his disciples. When he saw Jesus passing by, he said, "Look, the Lamb of God!"*
>
> *When the two disciples heard him say this, they followed Jesus. Turning around, Jesus saw them following and asked, "What do you want?"*
>
> *They said, "Rabbi" (which means "Teacher"), "where are you staying?"*
>
> *"Come," he replied, "and you will see."*
>
> *So they went and saw where he was staying, and they spent that day with him.* [81]

They went where Jesus went. They saw where he was staying. They spent the day with him. In fact, those two men (one was Andrew, as revealed in verse 40, and the other was probably John, who wrote the account but tended to mask his identity in his own accounts of events) became two of Jesus' closest followers. That was pretty much how it was done, as author Rob Bell explains in his book *Velvet Elvis*:

> *When a student applied to a rabbi to be one of his talmidim. . .if the rabbi believed that this kid [had] what it took, he would say, "Come, follow me."*
>
> *The student would probably leave his father and mother, leave his synagogue, leave his village and his friends, and devote his life to learning how to do what his rabbi did. He would follow the rabbi everywhere. He would learn to apply the oral and written law to situations. He gave up his whole life to be just like his rabbi.*
>
> *A friend of mine was in Israel a few years ago and saw a rabbi go into the bathroom and his talmidim followed him. They didn't want to miss anything the rabbi might say or do. This kind of devotion is what it means to be a disciple.* [82]

To follow Jesus is to go where he goes. John and Andrew went to where Jesus was staying. They spent the day with him. Over the next few years, they walked through Samaria with him. They slept on the floor beside him. They dined with him in the house of Zacchaeus, a notorious tax collector. They worshiped in the temple with him. They visited in the home of a Pharisee, where a disreputable woman washed Jesus' feet with her hair. They sailed the waters of Kinnereth with him. They went where he went.

For John, that eventually meant exile on the island of Patmos (where he received the revelation that is recorded and preserved as the last book of the New Testament). For Andrew, according to tradition, it meant a long, agonizing death by crucifixion at Patras in Achaea in Greece, as he hung on an X-shaped cross (at his request, because he felt unworthy to be executed in the manner of Jesus).

It means the same to follow Jesus today. It means to go wherever he goes, wherever he leads. It may mean striding the halls of academia. . .or washing the feet of those who do. It may mean risking the sneers and gossip of "religious" people in order to show mercy and grace somewhere that only Jesus would go. It may mean swallowing hard. Getting dirty. Risking infection. Enduring abuse. It will mean laying down your life, moment by moment, day after day. Because that's what it takes to go where Rabbi Jesus goes.

DO WHAT JESUS DOES

Dallas Willard, in his book *The Divine Conspiracy*, defined a disciple as "someone who has decided to be with another person, under appropriate conditions, in order to become capable of doing what that person does or to become what that person is." [83] He equates it to apprenticeship.

That is what Jesus means when he calls us to *follow* him. He doesn't intend for us to merely pray a prayer in order to go to heaven when we die. He doesn't mean for us to attend church services for an hour or two on Sunday and go our own way and do our own thing the rest of the week. When he calls us to follow, he expects us to be with him, day by day and moment by moment, in order to become capable of doing what he does and to become what he is. Willard continues:

> *What is it, exactly, that he, the incarnate Lord, does? . . .*
> *The answer is found in the Gospels: he lives in the kingdom of God, and he applies that kingdom for the good of others and even makes it possible for them to enter it for themselves. . . .*

[That] is what he calls us to by saying, "Follow me."

The description Peter gives in the first "official" presentation of the Gospel to the gentiles provides a sharp picture of the Master under whom we serve as apprentices. "You know," he says to Cornelius, "of Jesus, the one from Nazareth. And you know how God anointed him with the Holy Spirit and with power. He went about doing good and curing all those under oppression by the devil, because God was with him" (Acts 10:38).

And as a disciple of Jesus I am with him, by choice and by grace, learning from him how to live in the kingdom of God. This is the crucial idea. That means, we recall, how to live within the range of God's effective will, his life flowing through mine. Another important way of putting this is to say that I am learning from Jesus to live my life as he would live my life if he were I. I am not necessarily learning to do everything he did, but I am learning how to do everything I do in the manner that he did all that he did. [84]

When a man or woman follows Jesus in this way—intentionally, wholeheartedly, irrevocably—something amazing happens. Jesus referred to it—promised it, in fact—in his farewell address to his closest friends and followers:

"Very truly I tell you, whoever believes in me will do the works I have been doing, and they will do even greater things than these, because I am going to the Father." [85]

The person who breaks with the past, reorders his or her priorities, commits to going where Jesus leads and doing what Jesus would do will experience power to do "even greater things" through the empowering, indwelling presence of the Holy Spirit in his or her life.

"Even greater things?" Really, Jesus? It seems impossible. . .until we grasp the reality of Christ in us. Because he has gone to the Father, because he reigns on high, because he is exalted and holds all authority in heaven and on earth, there is nothing he cannot do. . .through you. Through me. Through the church. Through the company of those whose priority is to go where he leads and do what he will do, is doing, and wants to do. To such as those, "nothing will be impossible." [86]

THE FINAL WORD

The essence of following Jesus, as described in this chapter, is as follows:

- breaking with the past
- reordering priorities
- going where Jesus leads
- doing what Jesus would do

Before moving on to read the next chapter, discuss those four points with someone you can trust, and then answer the following questions:

1. Have I done each of these things?

2. Which is hardest for me?

3. Am I practicing these things on a daily basis? If so, how? If not, why not?

4. In what way(s) might God be nudging me to follow Jesus more intentionally, wholeheartedly, and irrevocably?

5

THE WORD THAT SATISFIES

My wife, Robin, and I recently celebrated thirty-six years of marriage. We don't look that old. At least, *she* doesn't.

One of the perks of being married all that time is that, for the last thirty-nine years (we dated for three years before we got married), neither of us has had to ask out anyone else (or *be* asked out) on a date. That is a blessing, because dating can be brutal. And it's even more brutal these days.

Back in the day ("olden times," as our grown children like to refer to our youthful days), a guy could ask a pretty girl for her phone number, and if she gave it to him, he was on his way!

Not so much anymore.

In fact, there is a relatively new service being offered these days. If someone asks for your phone number, you can smile politely and scribble down a legitimate number, and everyone's happy. . .until the caller dials the number and hears this message:

> *Thank you for calling. Unfortunately, the person who gave you this number does not want to talk to you or speak to you ever again. We would like to take this opportunity to officially reject you.*

That's pretty harsh, right? Some are even worse. One message says:

> *I'm sorry that you have to get this message from a complete stranger, but you have to know that you are a loser and no one will ever, ever love you.*

Somehow, the "I'm sorry" part rings a little hollow. Some of these services give you the option of rejecting someone in a male or female voice, gently or harshly, seriously or humorously, and in locations around the world.

It's awful. It's enough to make a person never, ever want to ask someone for a phone number again.

Because rejection is no fun. It's one of the most painful experiences we go through as humans. But it is also one of the most common. . .whether it's being picked last when kids are choosing sides on the playground, not being invited to a classmate's birthday party, being made fun of in middle school, not having a date for the prom, getting the call saying "we've hired someone else," being passed over for a promotion, or—if you're like me—dealing with the burden of having endured *all* those experiences!

It hurts, because we all want to feel accepted. We long to fit in. We crave a sense of acceptance and belonging.

THE GREATEST TRAP IN OUR LIVES

It is bad enough when we experience the rejection of others. I recently heard from a friend I've been praying for daily. He lost his job a couple of months ago and finally had a lead on a job that was perfect for him—his personality, his abilities, his experience. All the signs pointed in the right direction. Yet he wasn't hired. He texted me: "Rejection hurts."

It does. Even worse, it can lead us to believe what the voices of rejection seem to be saying. Henri Nouwen writes:

> *Over the years, I have come to realize that the greatest trap in our life is not success, popularity or power, but self-rejection. Success, popularity and power can, indeed, present a great temptation, but their seductive quality often comes from the way they are part of the much larger temptation to self-rejection. When we have come to believe in the voices that*

*call us worthless and unlovable, then success, popularity and
power are easily perceived as attractive solutions. The real
trap, however, is self-rejection. I am constantly surprised at
how quickly I give in to this temptation. As soon as someone
accuses me or criticizes me, as soon as I am rejected, left alone
or abandoned, I find myself thinking, "Well, that proves
once again that I am a nobody." Instead of taking a critical
look at the circumstances or trying to understand my own
and others' limitations, I tend to blame myself—not just for
what I did, but for who I am. My dark side says: "I am no
good. . . . I deserve to be pushed aside, forgotten, rejected and
abandoned."*[87]

Some of us have lived with those voices for so long that they sound like the truth. They sound like our own voice. They may even sound like God's voice.

But they're not.

God's voice speaks words of acceptance. Words that give. Words that restore.

THE WORD THAT ACCEPTS

The night before Jesus died, he gathered with his closest friends and followers in a borrowed banquet room in Jerusalem. There, in the custom of the day, he and his twelve disciples reclined on narrow couches, arranged like spokes on a wheel around a low table. The table was supplied with all they needed to share a Passover meal together. Matthew, one of the men who was there, recorded part of the evening:

*When evening came, Jesus was reclining at the table with
the Twelve. And while they were eating. . .Jesus took bread,
and when he had given thanks, he broke it and gave it to his*

disciples, saying, "Take and eat; this is my body."

Then he took a cup, and when he had given thanks, he gave it to them, saying, "Drink from it, all of you. This is my blood of the covenant, which is poured out for many for the forgiveness of sins. I tell you, I will not drink from this fruit of the vine from now on until that day when I drink it new with you in my Father's kingdom." [88]

When Jesus said, "Take and eat," he was doing several things at the same time. He was explaining the deep significance of the ancient ceremony they were sharing together. In the Passover, a lamb was eaten. Bread was broken. Wine was poured out. These things had been done for centuries as a way of remembering the first Passover, when God miraculously delivered his people from slavery and death in Egypt. When Jesus said, "Take and eat; this is my body," he was revealing the significance of the bread, which year after year had represented his body, which would soon be broken on a cross as he took on himself the punishment for the sins of the world.

But he was also doing something else when he said, "Take and eat." Just as he had done when he washed the disciples' feet just moments before, he was giving them a pattern to follow. Luke's account of the meal contains a detail that Matthew left out: "He took some bread and gave thanks to God for it. Then he broke it in pieces and gave it to the disciples, saying, 'This is my body, which is given for you. Do this to remember me.'" [89] Jesus told his followers to remember him in the breaking of bread, a command that is obeyed by his followers even today as they share a ceremony called Communion by some, or the Eucharist or the Lord's Table by others.

But even beyond the significance of those momentous acts, Jesus was doing one more thing. No one in that room but Jesus knew what that night would hold, and what the next day would bring: betrayal, denial, desertion, and more. But though Jesus knew enough to tell Judas to do what he planned and to warn Peter that he would fold under pressure, he still conveyed something to them all by breaking bread for them and sharing it with them. Author Brennan Manning explains:

> *In the Near East, to share a meal with someone is a guarantee of peace, trust, fraternity, and forgiveness: the shared table symbolizes a shared life. For an orthodox Jew to say, "I would like to have dinner with you," is a metaphor implying "I would like to enter into friendship with you." Even today an American Jew will share a donut and a cup of coffee with you, but to extend a dinner invitation is to say: "Come to my* mikdash me-at, *the miniature sanctuary of my dining room table where we will celebrate the most sacred and beautiful experience that life affords—friendship."* [90]

Even in the presence of his betrayer, Jesus extended acceptance to his friends. Though he knew Peter would soon deny him, Jesus held out a hand and shared his bread with him. To the men who—with one exception—would desert him in his hour of need, he offered friendship.

"Take," he said. It is a word he says to you. The word that accepts.

THE WORD THAT GIVES

On the first Easter Sunday, the day Jesus rose from the grave, a couple of his followers—not one of those who were in the upper room at the Last Supper, but a man named Cleopas and another (possibly Mary, his wife)—were walking along the road. The Gospel of Luke records what happened:

Now that same day two of them were going to a village called Emmaus, about seven miles from Jerusalem. They were talking with each other about everything that had happened. As they talked and discussed these things with each other, Jesus himself came up and walked along with them; but they were kept from recognizing him.

He asked them, "What are you discussing together as you walk along?"

They stood still, their faces downcast. One of them, named Cleopas, asked him, "Are you the only one visiting Jerusalem who does not know the things that have happened there in these days?"

"What things?" he asked.

"About Jesus of Nazareth," they replied. "He was a prophet, powerful in word and deed before God and all the people. The chief priests and our rulers handed him over to be sentenced to death, and they crucified him; but we had hoped that he was the one who was going to redeem Israel. And what is more, it is the third day since all this took place. In addition, some of our women amazed us. They went to the tomb early this morning but didn't find his body. They came and told us that they had seen a vision of angels, who said he was alive. Then some of our companions went to the tomb and found it just as the women had said, but they did not see Jesus."

He said to them, "How foolish you are, and how slow to believe all that the prophets have spoken! Did not the Messiah have to suffer these things and then enter his glory?" And beginning with Moses and all the Prophets, he explained to them what was said in all the Scriptures concerning himself. As they approached the village to which they were going, Jesus continued on as if he were going farther. But they urged him strongly, "Stay with us, for it is nearly evening; the day is almost over." So he went in to stay with them.

When he was at the table with them, he took bread, gave thanks, broke it and began to give it to them. Then their eyes were opened and they recognized him, and he disappeared from their sight. They asked each other, "Were not our hearts burning within us while he talked with us on the road and opened the Scriptures to us?"

They got up and returned at once to Jerusalem. There they found the Eleven and those with them, assembled together and saying, "It is true! The Lord has risen and has appeared to Simon." Then the two told what had happened on the way, and how Jesus was recognized by them when he broke the bread.[91]

Within hours of the resurrection, as Cleopas and his wife (who John says was one of the women who stood vigil at Jesus' cross[92]) trudged homeward after the Passover and tried to make sense of the horrific events of the past few days, Jesus appeared to them and engaged them in conversation. . .but "they were kept from recognizing him," Luke says. Even as Jesus explained the prophecies of scripture and how they were fulfilled in the events of his life—including, we may infer, his arrest, trial, crucifixion, and burial—they still didn't recognize him. Even when they opened their home to him and agreed to share their hospitality, they didn't see him for who he was.

But everything changed when "he took bread, gave thanks, broke it and began to give it to them."[93] Perhaps it was something in his manner when he took the bread. Maybe it was what he said when he gave thanks (though it was probably the standard Jewish blessing, "Blessed art thou, O Lord our God, King of the universe, who bringest forth bread from the earth"). Or it could have been something in the way he broke the bread, or perhaps all of those things combined.

But I think it is significant that Luke includes the detail that Jesus "began to give it to them." I think it is significant that it was in *that* instant—perhaps a second or two after they received the bread from his hand—that he disappeared from their sight. I think they became aware of the Lord's presence when their hands touched the bread.

Why was it that particular moment that he was revealed to them? I think it is because he wanted them to experience his grace in the breaking of bread. I think he wanted them to spread the news to all of his followers that his presence should be expected when they break bread together. And I think he wants us to receive his grace as easily, as freely, as frequently as we open our hands to take and as we open our mouths to eat.

"Take," he said. It is a word he says to you. The word of grace. The word that gives.

THE WORD THAT RESTORES
Just one more scene from Jesus' life. . .

Earle Ellis, in his commentary on Luke's Gospel, points out that the Last Supper in the upper room was the seventh time a scene in Luke's account involved a meal, and the scene in Cleopas's home in Emmaus is the eighth. Since the number seven often represents perfection and completion in Jewish thought and writing, Ellis suggests that the Last Supper scene symbolizes the completion of Jesus' redemptive work. In the meal Jesus shared with his two followers in Emmaus, therefore, "the symbolism identifies Jesus' resurrection as the beginning of a new creation."[94]

If that is so, the scene John describes at the end of his Gospel may add yet another layer of significance. John tells us that Peter and six other disciples had been out on the Sea of Galilee all night, casting their nets and catching nothing. Jesus appears along the shoreline, but—like the two disciples on the road to Emmaus—the disciples don't recognize him. However, when he tells them to cast their nets on the other side of the boat, resulting in a net-straining catch, Peter recognizes the Lord, swims ashore, and leaves the others to guide the boat to land. When they arrive, Jesus has a fire going and fresh bread on the coals. John continues the account:

Jesus said to them, "Come and have breakfast." None of the disciples dared ask him, "Who are you?" They knew it was the Lord. Jesus came, took the bread and gave it to them, and did the same with the fish. This was now the third time Jesus appeared to his disciples after he was raised from the dead.

When they had finished eating, Jesus said to Simon Peter, "Simon son of John, do you love me more than these?"

"Yes, Lord," he said, "you know that I love you."

Jesus said, "Feed my lambs."

Again Jesus said, "Simon son of John, do you love me?"

He answered, "Yes, Lord, you know that I love you."

Jesus said, "Take care of my sheep."

The third time he said to him, "Simon son of John, do you love me?"

Peter was hurt because Jesus asked him the third time, "Do you love me?" He said, "Lord, you know all things; you know that I love you."

Jesus said, "Feed my sheep. Very truly I tell you, when you were younger you dressed yourself and went where you wanted; but when you are old you will stretch out your hands, and someone else will dress you and lead you where you do not want to go." Jesus said this to indicate the kind of death by which Peter would glorify God. Then he said to him, "Follow me!" [95]

Once more, Jesus "took the bread and gave it to them." [96] He did the same with the fish. He did this, of course, after Peter had denied knowing him. He did this after Peter had deserted him. He did this after Peter had returned to his fishing boat in Galilee—even after he had seen the resurrected Jesus—perhaps assuming he would never again be trusted, that he would have no place in the kingdom, that his future held nothing more than boats and nets and fish.

But Jesus took the bread and—as he had in the upper room—held it out to Peter. He may even have said, "Take." And then he gave Peter the chance to assert his love for Jesus, three times—as many times as he had denied him. He told Peter that he would still be serving Jesus in the fairly distant future, and that rather than running away, he would be faithful to the end. And then Jesus repeated the words that began their adventure several years earlier, in effect reenlisting Peter in the kingdom cause: "Follow me."

I like to think that Jesus said, "Take," when he held out the bread to Peter. I believe it is a word he says to you and me. A word of restoration.

THE FINAL WORD

Take. Just one word. But Jesus says it to you just as he did to his earliest followers who gathered in the upper room. He knows your limitations. He not only knows how you have failed in the past; he knows how you will falter in the future. But he accepts you nonetheless. He calls you to his table, and he invites you to take.

You may be like those two disciples on the road to Emmaus. You may not know the scriptures as well as you think you should. You may feel foolish and slow to believe, as they were. But even so, Jesus says, "Take." He wants you to receive his grace as easily, as freely, and as frequently as you open your hands to take and open your mouth to eat. He wants you to know his grace as a daily, moment-by-moment gift. He wants you to receive from him and keep on receiving.

And before you protest that you are not worthy, that you have little to offer, that you—perhaps believing the words and feelings of rejection that have poisoned your past—have no illusions about your value to Jesus and his kingdom, remember Peter. Remember his humiliating collapse. Remember his disheartening failure. But remember also the word of restoration Jesus spoke to him.

And then *take*. Not just once. Not just weekly. But daily, moment by moment, breath by breath, bite by bite, do as Phillips Brooks suggested:

> *Feed on Christ, and then go and live your life, and it is Christ in you that lives your life, that helps the poor, that tells the truth, that fights the battle, and that wins the crown.* [97]

Take. Make an effort this week—and perhaps even for the rest of your life—to approach every meal as a reminder of Jesus' grace to you. As you take your first bite, whether it is bread or broccoli, hear his word of invitation: "Take." And in that moment, gratefully receive the word that accepts, gives, and restores.

THE WORD OF EXPECTATION

SCENE: *The Chat* television studio. The show's host and her guest are seated in two chairs on either side of a low table.

HOST: [to Camera One] Hello, and welcome to *The Chat*, where *we* talk, *you* listen, and everyone has fun! I'm your host, Fran Tastick, and our guest today has come from a long way to be with us. His name is Abraham, and he's from Ur. [Turning to guest] Did I say that right?

ABRAHAM: That is correct. Ur of the Chaldees. I was born in Haran. My father was Terah of Haran. His father was Nahor, whose father before him was Serug. His father was—

HOST: Yes, thank you. That will do. You're actually mentioned in the Bible, isn't that right?

ABRAHAM: Yes, that is true. I am mentioned in the first book of the Bible: *Bereshit*. Some people call it Genesis. I am also mentioned in Exodus, Numbers, Leviticus, Deuteronomy, Joshua, 1 Kings, 2 Kings, 1 Chronicles, 2 Chronicles, Nehemiah—

HOST: Fascinating, fascinating. Thank you. You're quite talkative, aren't you?

ABRAHAM: Well, yes, I guess you could—

HOST: I didn't mean for you to answer that.

ABRAHAM: Oh. Sorry.

HOST: I would like you to explain something, though. I'm told that the Bible holds you up as an example of faith.

ABRAHAM: I suppose you could say—

HOST: But what is faith, really? I mean, isn't it something different for each one of us?

ABRAHAM: I don't know about—

HOST: I mean, you believe what you believe, right? I believe what I believe. We both have faith.

ABRAHAM: I suppose you could—

HOST: So isn't it true that we can't really define faith in any absolute sense? I mean, isn't it a very personal thing?

ABRAHAM: You're quite talkative yourself.

HOST: But don't you agree?

ABRAHAM: Yes, it is a very personal thing, but no, I don't think it's at all hard to define.

HOST: Oh, really? Well then, how would you define [makes air quotes] "faith"?

ABRAHAM: Believing God.

HOST: Believing God? Doesn't that—

ABRAHAM: When God told me to leave Ur and said he would go with me, I believed him.

HOST: But that doesn't take into account—

ABRAHAM: When God told me I would have a son, and descendants as numerous as the stars in the sky, I believed him.

HOST: But you don't mean to suggest that—

ABRAHAM: I just believed him. And I didn't stop believing him, even when he told me to offer my son as a sacrifice on Mount Moriah. I couldn't imagine what he was thinking, and it was the last thing on earth I wanted to do, but I still believed him. I believed every word he ever said to me.

HOST: That seems like a rather simplistic approach.

ABRAHAM: You asked me a question; I answered it. [He gets up to leave.]

HOST: But if that's what faith is, then there are a lot of people around here—a lot of people in churches, even—who really don't have faith.

ABRAHAM: [Turns around, studies the host for a moment] You look like a nice young woman. So do yourself a favor, and listen to an old man. It doesn't matter what you say you believe. If my life teaches you anything, let it teach you this: What God speaks, you can believe. Where God leads, you must follow. What God asks, you must give. [Pauses] If you don't have that, you don't have faith. [Exits]

WHEN WORDS LOSE THEIR MEANING

It is called "verbal satiation" or "semantic saturation," among other things. It is the phenomenon we experience when we repeat a common word or phrase so often that it begins to sound strange and eventually seems to lose all meaning. Something like that has happened to the words *believe* and *faith*. Over time, through frequent use, perhaps—or, more likely, from misuse—those words have lost their meaning. Or they have come to mean something entirely different.

If Abraham heard us use those words in our twenty-first-century world, he would most likely be confused or amused. And Jesus, who claimed to be both Abraham's heir *and* predecessor,[98] must similarly shake his head when we use the words *faith* and *believe*. Because we use them in ways that would strike him as odd.

For example, the figures differ only slightly from year to year, but surveys routinely indicate that more than 90 percent of Americans *believe* in God, and 74 percent claim to have placed their *faith* in Jesus Christ. Think about those numbers. Is that what you see in your town? On your campus? In your neighborhood or workplace?

Yeah. Me neither.

You see, we tend to think of faith in narrow terms. "I believe in God," we say, or "I believe in Jesus." But what do we *mean* by that? That God—the God of the Bible—*exists*? That Jesus died on the cross for our sins?

James the apostle, in the Bible book that bears his name, made light of that kind of "faith," saying, "You believe that there is one God. Good! Even the demons believe that—and shudder."[99]

That is not what the Bible means when it says, "Abraham

believed God, and it was credited to him as righteousness."[100]

That is not what Jesus meant when he said, "For God so loved the world that he gave his one and only Son, that whoever believes in him shall not perish but have eternal life."[101]

One day, a man plunged through the crowd that surrounded Jesus and threw himself at Jesus' feet. "My little girl is at death's door," he said. "Please come and lay your hands on her and make her live."

Jesus agreed and turned toward the man's house. The crowd of onlookers and thrill seekers turned, too, and before long, Jesus stopped. He turned.

"Who touched me?" he asked.

"Who touched you?" asked one of his followers. "How can you ask that, with all the people jostling and crowding around you?"

He looked over their heads. "Who touched me?"

Then a woman came forward, her head bowed, her hands clasped, trembling, in front of her. She confessed that she had crept up behind Jesus to touch his *tzitzit*, the fringes on his clothing, in the belief that Jesus could, with a tiny touch, heal her long-standing, agonizing, debilitating health issues.

He nodded as if he knew her whole story. "Go in peace," he said. "You've been healed because you believe."

Even as he spoke to the woman, however, a messenger gripped the arm of the man who walked beside him. "No use bothering the rabbi any longer," he said. "Your daughter is dead."

Jesus shook his head and placed a hand on the man's shoulder. "Don't be afraid. Just believe."

When he arrived at the man's house, Jesus sent everyone outside and took the man and his wife—along with Peter, James, and John—inside. The girl, twelve years old, lay on a mat on the floor. Jesus stooped and lifted her hand.

"Little girl, get up," he said.

And she got up. She started walking around and even started interacting with the mourners at her own funeral.[102]

As Jesus left that place, two blind men stumbled after him, calling out, "Son of David, have mercy on us!" They kept calling as Jesus kept walking, and when he finally reached the home where he was staying, he let them catch up to him.

"Do you believe that I am able to do what you ask?" he said.

"Yes, Lord. We do!"

So he touched their eyes and healed them. "As you believe, so it is done."[103]

A desperate father. A sick woman. Two blind men. They came to Jesus. They believed. But what was the nature of their belief?

I think it was simple. Jesus didn't require a show of emotion. He didn't call for them to raise their hands or pray a particular prayer. He didn't ask them to believe a set of facts or doctrines *about* him. He asked them to believe *him*.

"BELIEVE I AM ABLE"

Do you remember the pointed question Jesus asked those two blind men? "Do you believe that I am able to do what you ask?"

That is what Jesus means when he says, "Believe."

"Believe I am able."

This explains his frustration with his closest friends and followers one day on the lake in Galilee:

One day Jesus said to his disciples, "Let us go over to the other side of the lake." So they got into a boat and set out. As they sailed, he fell asleep. A squall came down on the lake, so that the boat was being swamped, and they were in great danger.

The disciples went and woke him, saying, "Master, Master, we're going to drown!"

He got up and rebuked the wind and the raging waters;

*the storm subsided, and all was calm. "Where is your faith?" he
asked his disciples.*

*In fear and amazement they asked one another, "Who is
this? He commands even the winds and the water, and they
obey him."* [104]

To believe in Jesus is to trust his power. It is to rely on his
ability to save, heal, supply, sustain, and bless.

"BELIEVE I WILL"

In Jesus' day, there was no condition more frightening or pitiable
than leprosy. [105] A man or woman who was diagnosed with leprosy
faced a horrifying future. Bible scholar William Barclay describes
one form of the disease like this:

*It begins with an unaccountable lethargy and pains in the
joints. Then there appear on the body, especially on the back,
symmetrical discoloured patches. On them little nodules form,
at first pink, then turning brown. The skin is thickened. The
nodules gather specially in the folds of the cheek, the nose,
the lips and the forehead. The whole appearance of the face is
changed; the afflicted person loses all human appearance and
looks, as the ancients said, like a lion or a satyr. The nodules
grow larger and larger; they ulcerate and from them comes a
foul discharge. The eyebrows fall out; the eyes become staring;
the voice becomes hoarse and the breath wheezes because
of the ulceration of the vocal cords. The hands and the feet
also ulcerate. Slowly the sufferer becomes a mass of ulcerated
growths. The average course of the disease is nine years, and
it ends in mental decay, coma, and ultimately death. Those
suffering from this type of leprosy become utterly repulsive both
to themselves and to others.* [106]

This was the condition of one man who flung himself at Jesus' feet:

> *While [Jesus] was in one of the cities, there came a man full of leprosy. And when he saw Jesus, he fell on his face and begged him, "Lord, if you will, you can make me clean." And Jesus stretched out his hand and touched him, saying, "I will; be clean." And immediately the leprosy left him. And he charged him to tell no one, but "go and show yourself to the priest, and make an offering for your cleansing, as Moses commanded, for a proof to them."* [107]

Amazingly, though his condition was considered utterly incurable (and a medical cure for leprosy would not be found until the twentieth century), the leper believed that Jesus was *able* to heal him. "You can make me clean," he said. "You *can*."

The only question in the leper's mind was whether Jesus was *willing* to heal him. And Jesus answered, "I will."

To believe in Jesus is to trust his will. It is to believe him when he says, "I will never turn away anyone who comes to me." [108] It is to believe him when he says, "I will be with you always, to the end of the age." [109] It is to believe him when he says, "I will come again and will take you to myself, that where I am you may be also." [110]

"BELIEVE I AM"

There is an astounding passage in the eighth chapter of John's Gospel. Jesus sat on the "teaching steps" of the temple in Jerusalem, as did many rabbis. But the things he said on that single occasion were so bold and shocking that they nearly cost him his life right on the spot.

To begin with, he said, "I am the light of the world." [111]

When his detractors, the Pharisees, began to argue with him, he said, "You are from below; I am from above. You are of this world; I am not of this world. I told you that you would die in your sins, for unless you believe that I am he you will die in your sins."[112]

At least, that's how most translations of the Bible phrase his words.

He seemed to be baiting them. They got angrier and angrier, and then he said, "When you have lifted up the Son of Man, then you will know that I am he."[113]

Again, that's how most versions translate what he said.

But he continued, and the back-and-forth between Jesus and the Pharisees became more and more heated. They accused Jesus of being a Samaritan and having a demon, while they postured as "children of Abraham." Jesus countered:

> *"Your father Abraham rejoiced as he looked forward to my coming. He saw it and was glad."*
>
> *The people said, "You aren't even fifty years old. How can you say you have seen Abraham?"*
>
> *Jesus answered, "I tell you the truth, before Abraham was even born, I AM!" At that point they picked up stones to throw at him. But Jesus was hidden from them and left the Temple.*[114]

Though many English translations fill in a pronoun (*he*) that seems to be implied in these verses, in the original Greek New Testament, Jesus uses similar language three separate times in his exchange with the Pharisees. His statements in verses 24, 28, and 58 could be phrased like this:

> *"Unless you believe that I AM, you will die in your sins."*

> *"When you have lifted up the Son of Man, then you will know that I AM."*
>
> *"Before Abraham was born, I AM!"*

No wonder the Pharisees wanted to stone him; he could hardly have been clearer. He claimed to possess all the power, authority, and glory of God, the "I Am" who called Abram out of Ur, who revealed himself to Moses in the burning bush, who whispered to Elijah and stood with Shadrach, Meshach, and Abednego in the fiery furnace.

Though his words offended and incensed his enemies, nonetheless "many who heard him say these things believed in him."[115] They trusted his power. They trusted his will. But they did more than that. They trusted his nature.

And you can, too.

You can trust him as the one who said, "I am the bread of life,"[116] whose nature it is to provide and sustain life.

You can trust him as the one who said, "I am the light of the world,"[117] whose nature it is to dispel darkness.

You can trust him as the one who said, "I am the door of the sheep,"[118] whose nature it is to protect and shelter.

You can trust him as the one who said, "I am the good shepherd,"[119] whose nature it is to care and lead and guide.

You can trust him as the one who said, "I am the resurrection and the life,"[120] whose nature it is to banish sadness and impart abundant life.

You can trust him as the one who said, "I am the way, the truth, and the life,"[121] whose nature it is to drive away confusion, distraction, error, doubt, and death.

You can trust him as the one who said, "I am the true vine,"[122] whose nature it is to impart his divine beauty, grace, and vitality to your human heart and life.

To believe in Jesus is to trust his power. It is to trust his will. It is to trust his nature. So what does that mean, in practical terms? It means that when Jesus says to forgive "not seven times, but seventy-seven times,"[123] you believe that he can and will help you forgive over and over, because he has forgiven you!

It means that when Jesus says to love others, even your enemies, you believe he can and will give you that kind of love, because "God is love."[124]

It means that when Jesus says, "Do not worry about your life, what you will eat or drink,"[125] you believe him. You don't say, "But my job," "But the kids," "But what if. . .?" You trust his power, will, and nature. You believe that he can supply your needs, that he will take care of you, that the Good Shepherd will be with you and take care of you, come what may.

It means that when Jesus says, "Give, and it will be given to you. A good measure, pressed down, shaken together and running over, will be poured into your lap. For with the measure you use, it will be measured to you,"[126] you believe him. You trust his power, will, and nature. You don't measure your giving down to the penny, thinking that you worked hard for your money and can only afford to give so much, and if you give away too much you won't have enough at the end of the month; you give "a good measure," because you actually believe not only what Jesus says, but what he can do, what he wants to do, and who he is! You believe that he will provide, and that your giving will ignite his giving, and you'll receive back a good measure, pressed down, shaken together, and *still* running over.

THE FINAL WORD

To believe in Jesus means to trust his power, will, and nature to such an extent that you actually begin to do what he says. Even if a storm is raging all around, you don't give in to panic, because you believe that Jesus can calm the storm. Even if you face an uncertain future, you continue to hope and rejoice, because you believe that Jesus will never leave you alone. Even if your child is gravely ill, you don't have to fear, because you believe Jesus loves that child, too, because his very nature is love.

So the final word in this chapter comes in four parts:

1. Identify one area in your life where you have the most trouble believing Jesus.
2. Take some time to consider whether you have trouble trusting Jesus' power, will, or nature (it may be that you doubt more than one, or even all three).
3. Confess your doubt to Jesus in the spirit of the man who brought his demon-possessed son to Jesus, saying, "I believe; help my unbelief!"[127]
4. Ask Jesus to show you his power, will, or nature concerning that area, in such a way that your faith will be strengthened.

For example, you may doubt your salvation. You may wonder whether Jesus has really, truly forgiven your sin. As you think it over, you may realize that it is not Jesus' will or nature that you doubt, but his power—you think your sin is so dark and deep that he can't possibly forgive it all. So then you confess your doubt to him and ask him to show you his power to forgive even the worst sins imaginable. In that moment (or perhaps over the course of the next week), he may bring to your attention some of the sins he forgave in the Bible, such as David's adultery or Peter's denials. Or he may bring to mind the words of a worship song or hymn that speak directly to your doubt. Or he may bring someone across your path whose past was even darker than yours and whose sense of God's grace and forgiveness is full and complete. Or he may do something entirely different. . .but he will answer your prayer.

That is just an example, of course. You may identify something completely different, such as finances or health, as the area in which you have trouble believing Jesus. Whatever your particular challenge may be, it is possible to truly believe that Jesus is able. It is possible to trust his will. And it is possible to rely on his divine nature to such an extent that you begin to do what he says.

THE WORD THAT OPENS HEAVEN

There are seven billion people in the world. Seven *billion*.

You might think that, out of all those people, there might be someone—just one—who thinks or feels the way you do, someone who understands, who "gets" you, whose heart beats in tune with your heart, whose mind anticipates your thoughts, whose expressions mirror your emotions.

Maybe you've met that person. Maybe not.

Either way, you probably still feel sometimes as if no one really knows. . .or cares. . .or understands. It's part of the human condition.

You may be surrounded by thousands of people every day. You may live in a city of millions. You may sometimes feel awash in a sea of people, and yet it's as if no one really knows you, no one really understands you, not even your friends, not even your family.

It's not about romance or finding the love of your life. It's not about friendship or family. It's about our common human longing to connect with someone on a level we seldom—if ever—seem to touch. It's about a nagging sense of aloneness and alienation that all our gadgets and games won't relieve.

If you've ever felt that way, you're not alone.

I say that not only because there are many who harbor those kinds of feelings, but also because it is not God's desire for you to feel that way. He has created you with a great and wonderful capacity for connection and communion—not only with other people, but with him as well. And the sense of emptiness and estrangement you often feel is a symptom, not a disease. It is an indication that your heart and soul are not getting what you long for—and what God longs to give you.

The means to meet that desire and fill that emptiness is prayer.

PRAYER THAT FILLS YOU UP

Don't freak out. Don't turn the page. Don't give up just yet.

You've heard it all, of course. You've listened to sermons on prayer. You've read books about prayer. You've tried. You've failed. Just like the rest of us.

But there's no escaping the fact that Jesus said, "Pray." When he said "pray," however, he was saying something new. He was revising. He was revolutionizing. Because he commanded and modeled a kind of prayer that was different. Unique. A kind of prayer that opens heaven and fills the human heart.

It was different from the type of prayer his contemporaries knew. It was different from what his closest friends and followers practiced. So much so, in fact, that it piqued their curiosity: "One day Jesus was praying in a certain place. When he finished, one of his disciples said to him, 'Lord, teach us to pray, just as John taught his disciples.'"[128]

It was different, too, from the prayers a lot of us have heard in church—you know, the kind that are filled with a lot of "thees" and "thous," a bunch of fancy words and impressive Bible phrases thrown in. When Jesus said, "Pray," he wasn't talking about repeating the right phrases, or reciting something so many times, or reaching a certain level of consciousness—or *un*consciousness!

He had a different idea. He revolutionized prayer. He changed the rules. He did to prayer what Michael Jackson did to dancing, what Picasso did to painting, what Apple did to cell phones.

When Jesus' disciples came to him and said, "Lord, teach us to pray," they weren't saying, "We don't know how to pray." They had been praying all their lives—a minimum of three times a day, in fact. They were saying, "We've been watching you. We watch you go off by yourself. Sometimes we follow you and spy on you a little. And we listen to you pray. But you don't pray like we do. You don't pray like other rabbis. You don't pray like anyone we've ever known. To us, prayer is boring and tedious. It doesn't seem to do much for us. But you—when you pray, it seems like heaven opens and touches you and everything around you. It's like it fills you and fuels you. Like it refreshes and recharges you. So. . .teach us to do what *you* do! Teach us to pray. . .like you."

That's what they were asking. And so Jesus answered their plea. But he didn't respond with a seminar or a formula. He said, in effect, "Watch."

"Pray like this," he said.

> " *'Our Father in heaven!*
> *May your Name be kept holy.*
> *May your Kingdom come,*
> *your will be done on earth as in heaven.*
> *Give us the food we need today.*
> *Forgive us what we have done wrong,*
> *as we too have forgiven those who have wronged us.*
> *And do not lead us into hard testing,*
> *but keep us safe from the Evil One.*
> *For kingship, power and glory are yours forever.*
> *Amen.'* " [129]

You may know it as the Lord's Prayer or the Our Father. You may have recited it or heard it recited in church. It is a masterpiece of beauty and concision—which is what we would expect from the Son of God himself. It is not primarily a prayer to be recited and repeated; it is a pattern to guide our praying. It contains the main things Jesus wanted to teach his closest friends and followers about prayer. It encapsulates the ways he wanted them to pray. It succinctly and superbly expresses twelve ways he wants you and me to pray as well.

PRAY COMMUNALLY

In the famous Sermon on the Mount, Jesus instructs his followers:

> *"When you pray, you must not be like the hypocrites. For they love to stand and pray in the synagogues and at the street corners, that they may be seen by others. Truly, I say to you, they have received their reward. But when you pray, go into your room and shut the door and pray to your Father who is in secret. And your Father who sees in secret will reward you."* [130]

He made it clear that prayer is not a performance, but a conversation. It is not for showing off in public but for showing up in private. Interestingly, however, when Jesus gave his followers a pattern for prayer, he said to begin, "Our Father. . ."

"Our. . ."

Not "My. . ."

But "Our. . ."

He told them to pray, "*Our* Father. . .give *us*. . .forgive *us*. . .lead *us*. . .deliver *us*."

Of course, he may have used those terms simply because he was speaking to a group of people. But he still could have prescribed a pattern like the *modeh ani* ("I give thanks") prayer that he and his disciples (like observant Jews today) may have recited daily upon waking, while still in bed: "I give you thanks, living and eternal King, for you have returned my soul within me, with compassion. Great is your faithfulness."

But Jesus told his followers to pray, "*Our* Father. . ." It is a communal prayer. Even when it is prayed in private, in solitude, it is a corporate prayer, because one never prays alone.

The Bible says that when we pray, the Holy Spirit prays with us (Romans 8:26). We are surrounded by an invisible amphitheater of saints who are cheering us on (Hebrews 12:1), and our individual prayers, together with the prayers of all God's people, are presented before the throne of God by angelic hands (Revelation 8:3–4).

So when you pray, say, "Our. . ." Pray communally. Pray in the knowledge that you never pray alone. Pray with the awareness that you pray in harmony with your brothers and sisters around the world and throughout history.

PRAY RELATIONALLY

The men who said to Jesus, "Teach us to pray," were accustomed to praying, "Blessed art thou, Lord God, King of the universe," and "I give you thanks, living and eternal King." But Jesus said, "When you pray, say: 'Father. . .' "[131]

Their praying was proper, but Jesus' praying was *personal*. Relational. Intimate.

Jesus redefined prayer with a single word. He transformed it from ritual to relationship, from the way a slave might address a master to something more like a child climbing into a father's lap. In fact, the Bible says:

> *You have not received a spirit that makes you fearful slaves.*
> *Instead, you received God's Spirit when he adopted you as his*
> *own children. Now we call him, "Abba, Father."* [132]

> *Because we are his children, God has sent the Spirit of his Son*
> *into our hearts, prompting us to call out, "Abba, Father."* [133]

You who were once far off from God, who in fear and trembling could only address him as "Most High," "Holy One," "Lord and King" (all of which are totally proper and right to do), can nonetheless *now*—through Jesus—approach God not *only* as Lord and King, but also as loving, tender, gracious Father.

"Abba."

"Papa."

"Daddy."

It is impossible to overestimate how revolutionary this was in Jesus' day—so much so, in fact, that for Jesus to call God "Father" sounded blasphemous to the ears of his contemporaries. But Jesus went even further and told his followers to say, "Abba, Father," which means you can't be too relational, too intimate, too familiar, in prayer. You can be—should be—as personal and affectionate as a crying toddler seeking comfort or a young child asking for an ice cream cone.

PRAY CONFIDENTLY

Before proceeding with the Lord's Prayer, it is important to remember the intimacy of calling God our "Father," or it would be easy to misunderstand the next phrase that Jesus says to pray: "Our Father *in heaven*." This does not mean "Our Father who is far removed from us." Remember, Jesus has already told us to pray relationally and intimately, so his description of our Father as the one who is in heaven cannot possibly suggest that God is distant or unapproachable. Rather, it is an indication that we are to pray in the awareness that our Father, to whom we pray, is not a creature like us. He is not bound by the laws of nature. He is above all. He sees all, knows all, and controls all. He rules the universe.

He is the one whom Isaiah saw "high and exalted, seated on a throne."[134] He is the one whom the prophet Micaiah described as "sitting on his throne with all the multitudes of heaven standing around him on his right and on his left."[135] He is the one depicted in John the Apostle's vision as seated on a throne "suffused in gem hues of amber and flame with a nimbus of emerald."[136] He is the one who says of himself:

"My thoughts are nothing like your thoughts. . . .
And my ways are far beyond anything you could imagine.

For just as the heavens are higher than the earth,
so my ways are higher than your ways
and my thoughts higher than your thoughts."[137]

So when you pray, "Our Father in heaven," you can and should do so in utter confidence. Pray in the realization that your Father transcends the limits of this world, the limitations of creation. Pray with the understanding that what is impossible for you is totally possible for him. Pray in the awareness that your Father's "love has no limits, his grace has no measure, his power no boundary known unto men."[138] Pray in the knowledge that he is able to "do infinitely more than we can ask or imagine."[139] Pray confidently, because your Father is the one who is "in heaven."

PRAY RESPECTFULLY

Though Jesus invites and instructs us to pray relationally—to call God "Abba" and "Father"—he does not want familiarity to breed contempt, or intimacy to foster disrespect. He never wants us to forget that God is holy. He says to pray, "May your name be kept holy."

In Jesus' day, this meant that devout Jews would not even speak or write the name of God, lest they misuse it or profane it somehow. As a result, the pronunciation of the Hebrew name for God—YHWH, as it is spelled in English letters—has been lost; scholars can only guess at what vowels it contained and how it might have sounded. According to Dallas Willard, "The idea is that his name should be treasured and loved more than any other, held in an absolutely unique position among humanity."[140]

So Jesus says, in effect, "Don't lose that sense of awe and respect. Pray for God's name to be kept holy. Approach him that way. Respect him. Exalt him. Glorify him. Be glad that he is holy, and always pray for his name and nature to be honored and upheld by your prayers."

PRAY COOPERATIVELY

After Jesus instructs his followers to pray for God's name to be kept holy, he tells them to pray, "May your Kingdom come soon. May your will be done on earth, as it is in heaven."[141] That is, pray for God's rule to be realized and his will to be done as fully and expeditiously as it is in heaven itself. In other words, we do not pray in order to get God to join *our* cause; we enlist in *his* cause. We do not pray to get him to do what *we* want; we pray to align ourselves with *his* agenda.

Dallas Willard writes:

> *We are thinking here of the places we spend our lives: of homes, playgrounds, city streets, workplaces, schools, and so forth. These are the places. . .where we are asking for the kingdom, God's rule, to come, to be in effect. Also, we are thinking of our activities more than of those of other people. We know our weaknesses, our limitations, our habits, and we know how tiny our power of conscious choice is. We are therefore asking that, by means beyond our knowledge and the scope of our will, we be assisted to act within the flow of God's action.*
>
> *But we are also praying over the dark deeds of others in the world around us. We see how they are trapped in what they themselves often disown and despise. And we are especially praying about the structural or institutionalized evils that rule so much of the earth. . . . We therefore pray for our Father to break up these higher-level patterns of evil. And, among other things, we ask him to help us not cooperate with them, to cast light on them and act effectively to remove them.* [142]

It takes discernment to pray, "May your kingdom come, your will be done on earth as in heaven." When we pray those words, we must also seek God's guidance and listen for his voice. We need to ask as we pray, "Will this advance your kingdom? Does this prayer align with your will?" And when we are unsure, we can echo another of Jesus' prayers: "Not my will, but yours, be done."[143]

PRAY SPECIFICALLY

Jesus urged his followers to be specific in prayer. He suggested the petition, "Give us the bread we need for today."[144] He could have said, "Provide our needs." He could have said, "Take care of us." But he didn't. He said, "Give us our daily bread."

Samuel Logan Brengle writes:

> *Prayer must be definite. Once, when Jesus was leaving Jericho with his disciples and a great number of people, blind Bartimaeus sat by the wayside begging; and when he heard Jesus was passing by, he began to cry out, and say: "Jesus, thou Son of David, have mercy on me." But that prayer was not definite. It was altogether too general. Jesus knew what Bartimaeus wanted, but He desired Bartimaeus to state exactly what he desired, and said to him: "What wilt thou that I should do unto thee?" Then the blind man prayed a definite prayer: "Lord, that I might receive my sight." And the definite prayer there and then received a definite answer, for Jesus said unto him: "Go thy way; thy faith hath made thee whole," and immediately he received his sight (Mark 10:46-52).*
>
> *We should be as definite when we go to God in asking Him for what we want.* [145]

The pattern of prayer Jesus taught his disciples urges us to pray specifically. Pray for your children, not only by name, but according to their need: "Father, heal the burn on his finger," "Abba, give her peace and confidence in her job interview." Pray specifically for upcoming conversations, outgoing mail, overdue payments, and more. Tell God what you want; don't beat around the bush. As with Bartimaeus, God may know exactly what you need, but he may be waiting for you to think it through, figure it out, and speak it aloud. Then, when he answers, you will be quicker to recognize the answer as coming from him.

PRAY PRACTICALLY

There is another facet to Jesus' instruction, "When you pray, ask for bread." It wasn't only specific; it was also practical. In fact, it doesn't get much more practical than that.

The Autobiography of George Müller tells the story of a remarkable man of faith who, after some experience as a preacher, began a series of ministries—a Bible institute, Sunday school, orphan homes, and more—in Bristol, England. But that's not half the story.

Müller determined to show the church the outline and fruits of a life lived and a ministry run in complete and constant reliance on God. Month by month and year upon year, he resolutely depended on God for his (and hundreds of employees' and orphans') daily bread—quite literally at times. He determined from the beginning of his ministry that, rather than appealing to donors or fund-raising efforts for financial support, he would "take it to the Lord in prayer," as the hymn says, and await God's timing and God's supply. And time after time—often before he finished praying—he received answers to his prayers.

Here is a sample entry in his autobiography (which is composed of many of his journal entries), at a time when he and his staff cared for nearly a hundred children in three orphan houses:

> *The funds are now reduced to about twenty pounds. But thanks to the Lord, my faith is stronger than it was when we had a larger sum on hand. God has never at any time,*

from the beginning of the work, allowed me to distrust Him.
Nevertheless, real faith is manifested by prayer. Therefore,
I prayed with the headmaster of the Boys' Orphan House.
Besides my wife and brother Craik, he is the only person I
speak to about our financial status.

While we were praying, an orphan child from Frome was
brought to us. Some believers sent five pounds with the child.
Thus we received a timely answer to our need. We have given
permission for seven children to come in and plan to allow
five more. Although our funds are low, we trust that God will
meet our needs. [146]

Few people—if any—have ever prayed as practically as George Müller. . .or Bartimaeus. But we should. In fact, if we learned to "carry everything to God in prayer,"[147] as the hymn says, we would not only stop forfeiting peace and bearing needless pain; we would also reap great joy. We would stop erroneously seeing our food as coming from the grocery store and our paychecks as coming from an employer, and would recognize the true and constant supplier of all our needs: God, our Father.

PRAY CONTRITELY
Centuries before Jesus, his ancestor King David prayed:

My sacrifice, O God, is a broken spirit;
a broken and contrite heart
you, God, will not despise. [148]

Jesus instructs his followers to pray contritely in the phrase "Forgive us what we have done wrong."[149] Like the tax collector in the temple, who prayed, "God, be merciful to me, a sinner!"[150] and thus found favor with God, our prayers should include a posture of repentance, an attitude of humility, and a confession of sin. Dallas Willard presents it as a plea for pity:

> *Today. . .many Christians read and say "forgive us our trespasses" as "give me a break." In the typically late-twentieth-century manner, this saves the ego and its egotism. "I am not a sinner, I just need a break!" But no, I need more than a break. I need pity because of who I am. If my pride is untouched when I pray for forgiveness, I have not prayed for forgiveness. I don't even understand it.*
>
> *In the model prayer, Jesus teaches us to ask for pity with reference to our wrongdoings. Without it, life is hopeless. And with it comes the gift of pity as an atmosphere in which we then can live. To live in this atmosphere is to be able simply to drop the many personal issues that make human life miserable and, with a clarity of mind that comes only from not protecting my pride, to work for the good things all around us we always can realize in cooperation with the hand of God.* [151]

Pray contritely, Jesus says. Confess freely. And humbly receive the mercy and grace that are yours in Christ Jesus.

PRAY GRACIOUSLY

After urging his followers to pray contritely, Jesus does something artful and beautiful. In the next instant, after referring to the forgiveness we receive from God, he mentions the forgiveness we extend to others. The two are inextricably linked. We are forgiven; we forgive. This is how Jesus tells us to pray: "Forgive us what we have done wrong, as we too have forgiven those who have wronged us."[152]

Andrew Murray writes:

Scripture says, "Forgive one another, even as God also in Christ forgave you." God's full and free forgiveness should be the model of our forgiveness of men. . . . Our forgiving love toward men is the evidence of God's forgiving love in us. . . . The right relationships with the living God above me and the living men around me are the conditions for effective prayer. [153]

When Jesus says, "Pray," he means for us to pray graciously. We must pray not only *for* forgiveness; we must pray *in* forgiveness. If we cannot pray graciously (in an attitude of forgiveness toward others), we cannot pray contritely (in an attitude of repentance toward God). So in order to pray as Jesus says to pray, we must examine ourselves, as W. Phillip Keller suggests:

Do we really have a clear conscience in our relationship with other human beings? Is the atmosphere between me and my fellowman open and unclouded by hostilities? Do I still harbor old hates in my heart? Am I inclined to indulge in ill will over some hurt? Do I allow resentments to rankle beneath the surface of my life? Is there a gnawing grudge against someone tucked away secretly in the back of my memory? . . . Do the wrongs I have endured from others eat away inside me like a consuming cancer? [154]

We don't need to obsess over the possibility that we may be harboring some tiny seed of unforgiveness. Chances are, if we are harboring unforgiveness against someone, we know it. And if we are sincere in praying *for* forgiveness, we can ask the Holy Spirit also to help us pray *in* forgiveness. He may prompt us to go to a brother or sister and make things right before we can pray sincerely as Jesus tells us to pray; but his grace will go with us "as we also forgive those who have wronged us." [155]

PRAY SUBMISSIVELY

Depending on the phrasing of the Bible translation you use, it may be easy, in reading the Lord's Prayer, to miss the fact that it includes a prayer of submission. Many versions render the first part of verse 13, "And don't lead us into temptation." It is possible, however, to turn the first phrase into a positive, as the English Standard Version does: "And lead us not into temptation." Phrased in that way, those words are transformed into a prayer of submission, a plea for God to lead the surrendered soul.

It is a prayer like that of the hymn "Savior, Like a Shepherd Lead Us":

Savior, like a shepherd lead us, much we need Thy tender care;
In Thy pleasant pastures feed us, for our use Thy folds prepare:
Blessed Jesus, blessed Jesus! Thou hast bought us, Thine we are;
Blessed Jesus, blessed Jesus! Thou hast bought us, Thine we are.

We are Thine, do Thou befriend us, be the guardian of our way;
Keep Thy flock, from sin defend us, seek us when we go astray:
Blessed Jesus, blessed Jesus! Hear, O hear us when we pray;
Blessed Jesus, blessed Jesus! Hear, O hear us when we pray. [156]

Try it. Pray submissively. If you pray the Lord's Prayer, pause meaningfully after the words "Lead us." Make it a plea. Make it a moment of surrender. Make it a request for God to guide and direct you in your day, your decisions, and your life.

PRAY PURPOSEFULLY

Jesus says to pray, "Lead us not into temptation, but deliver us from evil."[157] This is not a suggestion that God leads us into temptation, for the Bible says, "God is never tempted to do wrong, and he never tempts anyone else."[158] It is, however, an acknowledgment that we need help to avoid temptation and to experience deliverance.

W. Phillip Keller helps us again:

> *It is tremendously encouraging for us to know that this*
> *petition can be answered positively. It inspires our spirits*
> *to realize that we can be delivered from evil and the evil*
> *one. It stimulates our souls and strengthens our resolve to be*
> *completely God's children. It is possible to sense the presence*
> *and power of Him who can save us from Satan and sin*
> *and our own selfish wills. We do not have to be enticed and*
> *trapped and tantalized by the enemy of our souls. We can*
> *be triumphant in temptation. To know this is to step out of*
> *despair into a delightful walk with our Father.. . .*
>
> *Let us never, never forget that our Father does not want*
> *to see us succumb to temptation. He does not want to see us*
> *fall. He does not want to see us down in despair, struggling*
> *with self, and stained by sin. He wants us, as His maturing*
> *children, to grow up in strength so we can walk serenely*
> *with Him in the beauty of a strong, unsullied, intimate*
> *companionship.* [159]

Jesus says, "Pray purposefully. Pray to steer clear of temptation. Pray to be delivered from evil. Pray to stay free from sin. Pray for daily deliverance. Pray for moment-by-moment freedom and purity. Pray for the blessing of walking serenely with God "'in the beauty of a strong, unsullied, intimate companionship.'"

PRAY WORSHIPFULLY

The final phrase in the Lord's Prayer as some have learned it is not found in the prayer Jesus taught. However, it was added to the prayer as early as the late first century or second century: [160]

"For kingship, power and glory are yours forever. Amen." [161]

It is a fitting conclusion to any prayer. It is not a petition, but a proclamation. It is a short worship hymn, a testimony that God is God, above all, and worthy of kingship, power, and glory.

The final words of the Lord's Prayer instruct us to pray worshipfully. Bow before God as King in your mind, heart, and life. Acknowledge his power over you, over all. And make sure you give him the applause he deserves.

Pray, Jesus says. But he does not insist that we memorize the pattern he provided (though many have). And he does not require us to pray it word for word (though there's nothing wrong with that) or every day (though some have found great blessing in doing so). Instead, he has modeled prayer for us—what it can be like, how it can sound, what it can do, and how it can bless.

He says, "Pray communally. Pray relationally. Pray confidently. Respectfully. Cooperatively. Specifically and practically. Contritely and graciously. Submissively. Purposefully. And worshipfully." That's the way he prayed. That's the way he teaches us to pray.

THE FINAL WORD

There are many versions of the Lord's Prayer—formal and informal, poetic and prosaic, simple and profound. The final word in this chapter is simply to choose a version that works for you and pray it once each day for the next week. You may wish to use your favorite Bible version (you'll find the prayer in Matthew 6:9–13 and Luke 11:2–4). You may want to Google "The Lord's Prayer" and find a favorite version online. You may want to write your own paraphrase or use one of these samples (the first is the author's paraphrase and the second is from the Holman Christian Standard Bible):

Our Father in heaven,
my Abba so close,
your name is great; may it be kept holy in all I pray,
all I say, and all I do.
Bring your kingdom to full fruition in my life
and in this world;
have your way here and now, just as you do in heaven.
Give us the things we need today.
Forgive our sins,
as we forgive those who have hurt us.
And lead us—
not into temptation—
but deliver us from evil and from the Evil One,
for you are our King,
and we welcome your reign,
and we exalt you forever and ever.
Amen.

Our Father in heaven,
Your name be honored as holy.
Your kingdom come.
Your will be done
on earth as it is in heaven.
Give us today our daily bread.
And forgive us our debts,
as we also have forgiven our debtors.
And do not bring us into temptation,
but deliver us from the evil one.
[For Yours is the kingdom and the power
and the glory forever. Amen.] [162]

THE WORD THAT FREES

A small closet occupies the space below the steps to our basement. For a while, my wife and I called it "the gift closet," because we used it for storing precious items we intended to give away as gifts. Nowadays, however, it does heavier duty than that.

Most of our Christmas decorations (except for the artificial tree we've used for more than twenty years) are in there. An 8mm home movie projector (the only thing other than a teacup and saucer that survives from my childhood). My wife's cornet (she has played it just once in the last twenty years but can't bring herself to part with it). A few items I hope to sell on Amazon. Oh, and one more thing: the kitchen sink.

Not literally, of course. But that closet has, over time, become the place for everything we don't have any other place for. Old DVDs (we no longer own a DVD player). Old handwritten family recipes we haven't transcribed or catalogued (and probably never will). Framed pictures that used to hang in our home. An inflatable mattress to which we've lost the pump. And more. Things just keep accumulating in there, and from time to time in the couple of decades we've lived in this house, I have cleaned out that closet.

And it feels so good.

It is one of my favorite things to do around the house. Honest. It probably sounds weird, but I thoroughly enjoy the feeling that comes when the undiscarded accumulation of years is pulled out to be given away or thrown out, and the only remaining contents of the closet are intentional, valuable, and worth keeping and organizing.

Our lives are like that. Our souls, even.

We don't intend for things to collect like they do. We didn't invite that cruel comment or hurtful slight. We never asked for that act of betrayal or broken relationship. We'd like to be rid of those sorts of things, but they hang around and, well, we don't always know where else to put them. So they linger. They cling. They accumulate.

They occupy space in our minds and hearts that would better be used for intentional, valuable, and positive things. They crowd out some of our freedom and joy. They wear on us. They drag us down. And if we don't clear them out, they can take over and cripple our lives.

That is why philosopher Hannah Arendt, in her study *The Human Condition*, says that the "faculty of forgiveness" is the only power that can stop the inexorable stream of painful memories and bring about true emotional healing. This is also surely one of the reasons Jesus speaks to us the word that frees. He says:

"Forgive us our sins, as we forgive those who sin against us." [163]

"If you forgive those who sin against you, your heavenly Father will forgive you." [164]

"Whenever you stand praying, forgive, if you have anything against anyone, so that your Father also who is in heaven may forgive you your trespasses." [165]

"Forgive, and you will be forgiven." [166]

Over and over again, Jesus says to us, "Forgive." He commanded it. He repeated it. He told parables about it. He made it a fundamental of faith in him, a litmus test of whether or not someone was a follower of his. But he did more than that. In the last moments of his life, he showed us the *how* and *why* of forgiveness.

THE PINNACLE OF FORGIVENESS

By the time Jesus arrived on the garbage heap the local people called Golgotha, or "Place of the Skull," the ways he had been mistreated must have seemed innumerable, incalculable.

His brothers and sisters had largely disowned him and showed no apparent concern in his hour of greatest need.

One of his closest friends had betrayed him. With a brotherly kiss on the cheek, even. For thirty pieces of silver, no less.

Another of his close friends had denied even knowing him.

His other *talmidim*—his twelve students, or disciples—had disappeared upon his arrest and, with one exception, hadn't lifted a finger—or even raised a voice—to defend him.

The religious authorities—the priests and Pharisees—had executed a vendetta against him. They had hounded him, lied about him, accused him of the most horrible things, and repeatedly tried to discredit him, frame him, and get him killed.

The politicians had seen him as a nuisance to be avoided. Or turned him into a pawn, a means of buying favor from each other.

All the people he had healed or fed or even raised from the dead? If they knew anything about his situation, they had done nothing.

The people of Jerusalem, who had hailed his arrival and talked incessantly about his actions and teachings for the last week? They either shouted "Crucify him!" or allowed their voices to be shouted down at the moment they counted most. Some had even watched him being led away to the place of crucifixion without a murmur of protest; the only person who helped him along the way was a foreigner, and even he had to be coerced into action.

He had been tried by an illegal court. Toyed with by a puppet king. Sentenced by a cynical governor. Brutally whipped and taunted by professional soldiers. Rejected by his own people. Deserted by all but his mother and a few close friends. And shamefully ogled by the mob.

So when he arrived at the place where he would die, the list of offenses against him—and the people who had committed the offenses—was immeasurable. Even then, however, there was more to come.

Someone—or more than one person—had to strip off his seamless robe and expose him, naked, to public view. Someone had to hold his hands against the patibulum, the heavy crossbar he had carried on his shoulders to the place of execution. Someone else had to pound the spikes that pierced his flesh. Others watched. Some taunted. Some of the crucifixion detachment even played games at his feet, gambling for his clothing.

Then it was that Jesus, having deserved none—absolutely none—of what he suffered, spoke from the cross that would soon claim his life: "Father, forgive them, for they know not what they do."[167]

Though his body was racked with pain, his heart broken from betrayal and rejection, and his mind clouded by pain, he nonetheless pronounced forgiveness, and prayed it, for all who had hurt him.

"Father, forgive them, for they know not what they do." Ten words in English. Only eight in Greek. Yet those few words reveal the infinite, gracious love of Jesus Christ and instruct us in the word that frees.

RECOGNIZE THE OFFENSE

One of the reasons forgiving can be so hard is because it means we must face the wrong that has been done to us. Some of us run so hard and fast from conflict that we don't want to face the fact that someone has hurt us.

Maybe because it means admitting that my mom and dad weren't perfect. Maybe because it feels wrong somehow to admit that my husband is an abuser or my friend acted selfishly or my pastor did something wrong or that God himself disappointed me.

Maybe because I am not about to give that person the satisfaction of knowing he hurt me, or maybe because if I face the wrong that was done I might have to pursue biblical reconciliation, and I don't want to. It scares me, or it's too much work, or something similar.

But if I'm going to avoid the soul-eating cancer of unforgiveness in my life, I've got to face the wrong that's been done to me. Not only that, but sometimes the process of forgiving someone who has wronged me will mean facing my own responsibility. It may mean coming to grips with the part I may have played—any wrongs I may have committed—toward the person who hurt me. It may mean facing the fact that the hurt I don't deserve is mixed in with some hurt I *do* deserve. It may mean facing the need to forgive myself as a first step toward forgiving someone else. But Jesus says to forgive, and he never commands us to do something we have no control over. So forgiving means to decide, to will, to let go of the wrong that has been done to me. To throw out the scorecard. To erase the debt.

Does that sound too hard? It can seem so. But sometimes it helps to make a symbolic gesture that will help bring our emotions into line with our will. Like writing down the wrongs we choose to forgive and then burning or shredding them as a way of releasing them. Or burying a hatchet, the way some American tribes did—just don't mark the spot so you can come back later and dig it up!

We seem to think that withholding forgiveness will make us feel better. . .even though our own experience tells us otherwise. We've been withholding forgiveness, and withholding, and withholding, and we're still miserable, still struggling, still flailing, still trying to move on, still trying to figure out why we don't get better and only seem to get worse, as if something is eating away at our happiness, our hope, and our spiritual strength.

Or we think that forgiving means ignoring or making little of the wrong that was done. It feels like excusing something that shouldn't be excused. But it is actually quite the opposite.

Scot McKnight, in his book *The Jesus Creed*, writes:

> *There can be no genuine reconciliation or forgiveness until a person confronts "who did what." Shoving an abusive situation into a hidden pocket of the heart only lets it fester until it abscesses. The victim meets the offender and the offense by naming it what it really is: stealing, sexual abuse, fraud, etc. The offense is a moral wrong, and it is not minimized by an effort to reduce the pain or hurry a reconciliation.* [168]

Forgiveness does not minimize a wrong; it recognizes it. It doesn't treat the harmful action as insignificant; by affirming that someone needs to forgive, and someone needs to be forgiven, it acknowledges and names the offense.

When Jesus prayed on the cross, "Father, forgive them," he recognized that wrongs had been done and sins had been committed—against him and against the Father. You and I do the same when we forgive, because where there is no wrongdoing there is nothing to forgive.

TRY TO SEE THINGS FROM THE OFFENDER'S PERSPECTIVE

The words of Jesus on the cross—"for they know not what they do"[169]—display a truly divine sense of empathy and compassion. While suffering the worst treatment the world could devise, Jesus saw from the height of Calvary that his betrayers, persecutors, tormentors, and executioners didn't understand what they were doing. He saw things not only from a heavenly perspective; he saw things from his offenders' perspectives.

So, too, when you are harmed in some way, Jesus teaches you to try to see things from the offenders' perspective. Do they know what they have done? Can they know how much they've hurt you? Did they act out of malice? Ignorance? Misunderstanding? Wrong information? Something else?

Novelist Harper Lee, in the classic novel *To Kill a Mockingbird*, portrays a conversation between the narrator, Jean Louise "Scout" Finch, and her father, Atticus Finch:

> *Atticus stood up and walked to the end of the porch. When he completed his examination of the wisteria vine he strolled back to me.*
>
> *"First of all," he said, "if you can learn a simple trick, Scout, you'll get along a lot better with all kinds of folks. You never really understand a person until you consider things from his point of view—"*
>
> *"Sir?"*
>
> *"—until you climb into his skin and walk around in it."* [170]

In order to forgive people, it helps to see the world through their eyes. Try to consider things from their point of view. Try climbing into their skin. Walk around in it.

You may discover that the people who hurt you don't know what they did. You may learn that they themselves are hurting, and that people who are hurting tend to hurt other people. You may come to realize that the offenders have been hurt as much by their actions as you were. Or you may discover something else entirely. But as Jesus showed us on the cross, the process of forgiving others can be helped along if we try to look beyond the hurt and see the situation from the perspective of the other person.

PRAY FOR THE OFFENDER

Have you ever had the wind knocked out of you? Maybe you fell off of something onto your back or got punched in the gut. Maybe you ran into something with such force that it knocked you backward, and for a few panic-stricken moments, you couldn't breathe. In medical terms, what happened was that the blow caused a spasm in your diaphragm, the muscle under your rib cage, basically paralyzing your breathing apparatus.

Something similar often happens when we are hurt—especially when we are hurt deeply. We may not stop breathing, but we may find that our pain makes it difficult to pray—and if we do pray, we want to pray for fire and brimstone to fall on the person or people who hurt us.

But Jesus showed us a better way. He modeled prayer for the offenders. For the Father to have mercy on them and forgive them. It was an example that clearly had an influence in the early church, because we see virtually the same attitude in Stephen, the first martyr of the church.

Stephen was preaching a sermon in Jerusalem—the city where, just weeks earlier, Jesus had been executed—and his listeners began to get upset at his blunt language:

> *The Jewish leaders were infuriated by Stephen's accusation, and they shook their fists at him in rage. But Stephen, full of the Holy Spirit, gazed steadily into heaven and saw the glory of God, and he saw Jesus standing in the place of honor at God's right hand. And he told them, "Look, I see the heavens opened and the Son of Man standing in the place of honor at God's right hand!"*
>
> *Then they put their hands over their ears and began shouting. They rushed at him and dragged him out of the city and began to stone him. His accusers took off their coats and laid them at the feet of a young man named Saul.*
>
> *As they stoned him, Stephen prayed, "Lord Jesus, receive my spirit." He fell to his knees, shouting, "Lord, don't charge them with this sin!" And with that, he died.* [171]

Stephen, like his Master, prayed for those who killed him. And we can profit from his example and from that of the Lord Jesus.

You probably won't *want* to pray for the person who hurt you; do it anyway. It may be hard at first; do it anyway. You may feel strange. You may feel like a hypocrite, praying words you don't really mean. You may have trouble thinking of something you can pray sincerely. Do it anyway.

If you follow the example of Jesus and pray for those who hurt you, you will soon be able to pray more sincerely. You will feel God's blessing pour into your heart. Your prayers will advance the process of forgiveness and freedom, and you will experience what Jesus said in the Sermon on the Mount:

> *When someone gives you a hard time, respond with the energies of prayer, for then you are working out of your true selves, your God-created selves.* [172]

FORGIVE PREEMPTIVELY

Scot McKnight points out that, in the Old Testament, "God's gracious forgiveness is center stage, but we don't find a challenge for humans to forgive. . . . Forgiveness, in the Old Testament, is a 'God thing.' "[173] But he also points out something else. Until Jesus came along, forgiveness was also a "repentance thing." That is, forgiveness followed repentance. If someone didn't say, "I'm sorry," then there was no forgiveness.

Fast-forward to Calvary. Jesus, on the cross, prays, "Father, forgive them, for they know not what they do."[174] For people who had "done him wrong," so to speak, and yet had not said—and may *never* say—"I'm sorry." He forgave. . .preemptively.

Like Jesus, you may sometimes be called upon to forgive people who don't know what they've done. Who may never fully grasp how they hurt you. Who haven't said—and may *never* say—"I'm sorry."

It's hard enough to forgive someone who asks for forgiveness.

But to forgive someone who hasn't asked? That is harder still. In fact, it may only be possible with Christ's help. Offering this kind of Christlike forgiveness is immensely freeing. What McKnight calls "preemptive strikes of forgiveness"[175] set us free from anyone else's timeline. They free us from the limits of anyone else's understanding. They free us to move forward instead of waiting—consciously or subconsciously—on our offender. They free us to forgive like Jesus—graciously, magnanimously, unconditionally.

FORGIVE AS OFTEN AS NECESSARY

There is no evidence that Jesus prayed, "Father, forgive them," more than once. Of course not. When Jesus forgives, it is a done deal. That's one of the perks of divinity, I think.

In fact, the Bible says that when God forgives, he forgets.[176] It says that when God forgives his people's sin, no amount of searching will ever find them again.[177]

But we are not like that. Our will does not fully control our memory. Our emotions can often get the better of us. So, for us, forgiveness must be a daily decision.

When the enemy of your soul, the devil, whispers in your ear and reminds you how someone hurt you, you may be surprised at the reappearance of old wounds. You may say to yourself, "I thought I forgave that person." You may even start to feel guilty for those old feelings returning.

Don't.

It is a part of the process. It is a common, frequent stop on the highway of forgiveness. It simply means that the hurt you suffered was significant. In fact, the deeper the hurt, the more often you will have to exercise your powers of forgiveness. And the longer it may take before your task is done.

So you must go on forgiving. Day by day, week by week, month by month. And as you do, the healing that follows forgiveness will place a growing distance between you and the thing you've forgiven.

It's a little like setting a toy boat into a flowing stream or river. Once you release the boat into the current, it will be taken farther and farther away until, sometime in the future, you'll lose sight of it.

That's what can happen when you forgive someone. Once you let go of the wrong that was done to you, the current of forgiveness will take the memory farther and farther away until you eventually lose sight of it and are fully and finally free, because the offense is fully and finally forgiven.

PURSUE RECONCILIATION IF POSSIBLE

In *The Jesus Creed*, Scot McKnight makes a helpful distinction between two kinds of forgiveness:

> *I believe there are two fundamental dimensions of forgiveness that need to be distinguished: objective forgiveness and subjective forgiveness. "Objective forgiveness" refers to the elimination of the offense in the relationship, that is, it refers to "reconciliation." The "subjective" includes both a disposition to forgive and an experience of forgiving: release of anger, hatred, and resentment—ending the internal recycling of the offense.* [178]

Jesus offered both objective and subjective forgiveness. With his prayer on the cross, he demonstrated subjective forgiveness— the release of anger, hatred, and resentment. With his death, he offered the possibility of reconciliation to all:

> *God. . .reconciled us to himself through Christ and gave us the ministry of reconciliation: that God was reconciling the world to himself in Christ, not counting people's sins against them. And he has committed to us the message of reconciliation.* [179]

We are likewise called to pursue both subjective forgiveness and objective forgiveness—that is, reconciliation. This means that when it is possible and appropriate, we *communicate* our forgiveness to the other person and *pursue* a restoration of the relationship. This often takes time, of course, and is not always possible. We should not expect a restored relationship to be "the same as it was," but we can hope for it to be good, perhaps even better. And we should keep in mind that, as McKnight says, "the degree of reconciliation is shaped by other factors: our hurts, whether or not the offender has repented, how long the offender may have served time in prison, if the offender is a dangerous person, if the offender is even alive, etc."[180]

Whether full reconciliation is possible or not, it is nonetheless possible and preferable, with God's help, to do as Scripture says: "Do all that you can to live in peace with everyone."[181]

AWAKE TO FREEDOM

In the last moments of his earthly life, Jesus prayed, "Father, forgive them, for they know not what they do."[182] Sometime later, he prayed, "Father, into your hands I commit my spirit."[183] And then he died. Those prayers—a prayer of forgiveness and a prayer of surrender—form a fitting prelude to the events of the coming Sunday morning, when he burst the bonds of death and strode from the grave in the freedom and beauty of the resurrection.

That picture can serve as a metaphor for people who have prayerfully forgiven those who have hurt them, just as Jesus did on the cross. They can look forward to a moment when, bursting the bonds of anger and pain, they awaken to a new morning of freedom and beauty in their lives.

When we forgive those who have hurt us and sinned against us, we will invariably find that we were the captive, not our offender. We will find that our forgiveness sets us free as it sets others free.

We will find healing and wholeness blooming in our hearts and minds as we pray for healing and wholeness in the lives of others, even those who have hurt us. And we will discover that we have changed our future by forgiving the past.

THE FINAL WORD

Frederica Matthewes-Green writes feelingly of the annual Rite of Forgiveness, which takes place at the beginning of Lent in Orthodox churches:

> *At last we reach the Rite of Forgiveness. As vespers comes to a close, the members of the church form a large circle. At the end nearest the altar the two ends overlap, as a subdeacon turns to face my husband, the priest. He bows to touch the ground, honoring the image of God in this person, then stands to say, "Forgive me, my brother, for any way I have offended you." After the subdeacon says, "I forgive you," he too bows to the ground, and asks for and receives the same forgiveness, and then the two embrace. Each of them then moves over to the next person in line. Over the course of an hour or so, every single person in the church will stand face-to-face with every other person. Each will bow to the ground and ask for forgiveness; each will bestow forgiveness on the other.*
>
> *As my husband says, "When we do this, we do something the devil hates." Teenaged brothers and sisters forgive each other. Small children solemnly tell their mothers, "I forgive you." Folks who have been arguing about the church budget for months embrace with tears.*
>
> *In fact, tears are the common coin of the evening. Some weep hard as they look in each face and think how they have slighted, ignored, or resented this person during the year—a person now revealed as bearing the face of Christ. Some weep*

> *as they are forgiven, over and over, in a nearly overwhelming*
> *rush of love and acceptance. Some weep and hug so much they*
> *hold up the line, but no one minds. A toddler is ignoring*
> *the line and going on his own steam from person to person,*
> *tugging on a skirt hem or trouser leg and looking up to ask,*
> *"Forgive?"*
>
> *This is how Lent begins for us. It's an exhilarating kick-*
> *start for a time that will get much harder. The number of*
> *services during Lent increase dramatically—during Holy*
> *Week there are eleven—and they get longer as well. Food*
> *simultaneously gets shorter. Old knees don't like prostrations.*
> *In all this, though, we rejoice; we look forward to Lent as a*
> *time that is invigorating and challenging. In the company of*
> *our friends we can run this race. It is good that it begins with*
> *forgiveness.* [184]

More churches should do that. More individual Christians, too, including you and me. So the final word for this chapter is to observe your own Rite of Forgiveness. One way to do that is this: At least once each day, pray the "forgive them" prayer of Jesus for someone who has hurt you. Your heart may not be in it at first. It may take some time for your emotions to catch up to your words and your will. But pray it anyway: "Father, forgive them (him, her), for they know not what they do." Pray it in faith. Pray it with abandon. Pray it until you mean it. Pray it as often as necessary. Pray it until you awake in freedom.

THE WORD ON WHICH
ALL WORDS HANG

Scientists of all kinds say it: human beings need love. We not only need to receive love; every one of us is wired from birth to give love, too. As trees are created to generate oxygen, and bees are engineered to produce honey, so you and I are equipped and driven to emanate love.

This may be part of the reason we use the word *love* in so many different ways. Not only do I *love* my wife, my kids, and my grandkids, but I also *love* Shakespeare. I *love* baseball. I *love* Oreos. I *love* reading. I *love* singing. I *love* hiking in the woods. I *love* the smell of freshly cut grass. I *love* massages. I *love* rock 'n' roll (put another dime in the jukebox, baby).

And you would *love* it if I stopped now, wouldn't you?

But you get the idea. We not only have a need to receive love; we need to give it, too. We are driven to love. Even the most self-absorbed person looks for opportunities to bestow love on something or someone else from time to time. It is why we can't resist puppies and kittens. It is why some old ladies are compelled to pinch children's cheeks. It is why we grieve when a celebrity we never met dies. It is why Julie (and others) in the musical *Show Boat* sing, "Fish gotta swim, birds gotta fly, I gotta love one man till I die."[185]

Jesus comes to us in our need and speaks the word on which all other words hang. He says,

> " 'Love the Lord your God with all your heart and with all
> your soul and with all your mind.' This is the first and greatest

commandment. And the second is like it: 'Love your neighbor as yourself.' All the Law and the Prophets hang on these two commandments." [186]

"Love," he says. And then he says something that would have surprised his listeners, something we so easily forget—or ignore: "Everything hangs on this."

Love. It is the word on which all other words hang.

Would you obey God's law? Jesus says, "Love."

Would you heed the words of the prophets? Jesus says, "Love."

Would you be great? Jesus says, "Love."

Would you be good? Jesus says, "Love."

As E. Stanley Jones points out, "There are 32,000,000 statutes on the statute books of America to make people good. The Christian has only one: 'Thou shalt love.' " [187] As Paul, the great church planter of the first century, said, "Love is the fulfillment of the law." [188] Love is the target at which the Law and the Prophets aim. Love is the point. Love is the objective. Love is the destination.

But who are we to love? And how? And to what extent? In giving us the word on which all other words hang, Jesus answers those questions.

LOVE GOD

When Jesus spoke the word on which all words hang, he was answering a question. A trick question, in fact. The incident, as recorded in Matthew's Gospel, happened this way:

Hearing that Jesus had silenced the Sadducees, the Pharisees got together. One of them, an expert in the law, tested him with this question: "Teacher, which is the greatest commandment in the Law?"

Jesus replied: "'Love the Lord your God with all your

*heart and with all your soul and with all your mind.' This is
the first and greatest commandment. And the second is like it:
'Love your neighbor as yourself.' All the Law and the Prophets
hang on these two commandments."* [189]

In his answer to his antagonists, Jesus was not saying anything
original at all. He was quoting the Torah—specifically, the *Shema*,
the central, fundamental, defining words of Judaism:

> *Hear, O Israel: The* LORD *our God, the* LORD *is one. Love the*
> LORD *your God with all your heart and with all your soul and
> with all your strength.* [190]

Nor was Jesus being creative in identifying those words as the
greatest commandment. He was echoing the opinions of other
rabbis, such as Hillel, who lived around the same time as Jesus and
said much the same thing in answer to a similar question.

Jesus was also not being controversial in identifying love for
God as the greatest commandment. In fact, it probably would have
been controversial if he had *not* said that the most important thing
we can do in life, the greatest obedience we can offer to God, is to
love him with all our heart, soul, mind, and strength.

As conventional as his answer was, however, it was—and is—a
largely ignored command. Like the Pharisees, we generally excel at
fearing God, but our fear (or *respect*, if you prefer) is not a product
of love. Like the Pharisees, we take pains to obey God (and
pressure others to obey him or judge them when they don't), but
our obedience is not a free-flowing expression of love. We worship
and pray and read our Bibles, but more often out of obligation
than out of love.

But loving God, according to Jesus, comes first. It is first in
importance and first in sequence. It is the word on which all other

words hang. It is the action from which all other actions should proceed.

Love is sort of like tupelo honey, which, according to the Savannah Bee Company (and others), is "the gold standard by which other honeys are measured."[191] Tupelo honey is produced by bees in areas where tupelo trees grow (primarily in the southern United States). When bees gather nectar from tupelo trees, the sweetness of the nectar is reproduced in the honey, lending it a distinct and prized appeal. Something similar happens in people who love God with all their heart, soul, mind, and strength. The sweetness of that love produces a unique and beautiful kind of reverence, obedience, and devotion that is unlike the outwardly similar varieties that arise from fear, obligation, or routine.

"Love," Jesus says. "Love God. Love him first. Love him foremost. Love him fully."

LOVE ALL

Jesus said that the greatest commandment is to love God with all you've got. But he didn't stop there. The second most important commandment, Jesus said, is the spittin' image of the first. It is what the first commandment sees when it looks in the mirror. It is the chip off the old block. It is "Love your neighbor as yourself."

Of course, when Jesus said that the second commandment was like the first, he was no longer answering the question he had been asked. Did you notice that?

The Pharisees asked him what he considered the *greatest* commandment. He could have said, "Love the LORD your God with all your heart and with all your soul and with all your strength," and left it at that. No one would have been surprised. No one would have been disappointed, except maybe the Pharisees, who were hoping he'd dig himself a hole in which they could stone him. But he didn't. He kept talking. He gave them a bonus answer. A two-for-the-price-of-one. A BOGOF.[192]

The "second greatest commandment" may have been a mild surprise to his listeners, because Jesus lifted that command from a more obscure location, from Leviticus 19:18, which says, "Do not seek revenge or bear a grudge against anyone among your people, but love your neighbor as yourself.[193]

He passed over a whole lot of other commandments to get to that one—such as "do not steal," "do not lie," "do not turn to idols," and more. He passed over prohibitions against taking the Lord's name in vain and eating pork. He passed over commands about fasting and keeping the Sabbath.

But if his words raised any eyebrows, they wouldn't have dropped any jaws, because these, too, were substantially the same things Rabbi Hillel said in a similar situation. The truly surprising part—scandalous, in fact—would have been how Jesus *applied* the two greatest commandments.

When Jesus said, "Love your neighbor," the people may have thought to themselves, *Oh, okay,* and applied the command to their *closest* neighbors, the members of their own household. After all, who wouldn't agree that anyone who loves God should love his or her own family?

Some of his listeners may have been generous enough to give his words a broader application in their minds. When Jesus said, "Love your neighbor," they may have thought to themselves, *Oh, sure,* and applied the command to their friends as well, because obviously God wants us to have friends, and we should love those friends, right? Like Mama said, "If you want to have a friend, you've got to *be* a friend."

A few of Jesus' listeners might have been even more magnanimous. When Jesus said, "Love your neighbor," they may have thought to themselves, *Oh, well,* and applied the command beyond their family and friends. . .to "people I like." They may not be friends, but they're likable. They're pleasant, they say hi when we pass on the street. Certainly it is a "mitzvah," a righteous act, to love people like that. You know, people who don't litter, who don't cut us off in traffic, who don't take too long to order at Starbucks. It's possible that *some* of Jesus' listeners that day might have been willing to go that far.

But when Jesus said, "Love your neighbor," no one would have applied the command beyond that. Not even Jesus' closest followers would have thought when he said, "Love your neighbor as yourself," that he could possibly be talking about, you know, *people who aren't like me.* Not a single one of them would have thought he could mean someone who wasn't righteous. . .and surely not someone who wasn't Jewish. . .certainly not someone who was of another race. . .nation. . .or culture. After all, those people who heard Jesus speak the word on which all other words hang would have assumed—just as we would—that you can't really love someone you don't get, right? You can't love someone who's totally unlike you. You can't love a person who is clearly—even intentionally—separate and "other" from you. Right? You can't love those who look down on you, or curse you, or demonstrate against you, or want to hurt you, or stand for things that completely contradict what you stand for. Right?

No one would have applied the command beyond that. . .until *that guy* spoke up. You know the one. The kid in class who thought he had all the answers. The one who messed up the curve for everyone else. The one who kept everyone else from being dismissed early by actually asking a question when the teacher said, "Any more questions?"

The Gospel of Luke records that "on one occasion an expert in the law stood up to test Jesus. 'Teacher,' he asked, 'what must I do to inherit eternal life?' "[194]

It may have been on the same occasion that Matthew records

("an expert in the law" is synonymous with "Pharisee"). It may have been some wise guy's further attempt to trip up Jesus after the question about the greatest commandment had failed to produce the desired results. Or it may have been a totally separate conversation, albeit one that perfectly follows Jesus' words to "love God, love all." Luke's account continues:

> *"What is written in the Law?" [Jesus] replied. "How do you read it?"*
>
> *He answered, " 'Love the Lord your God with all your heart and with all your soul and with all your strength and with all your mind'; and, 'Love your neighbor as yourself.' "* [195]

It seems that this "expert in the law" thinks he's being really smart. Like that guy we all knew in school, he has learned to parrot exactly what the teacher just said. He probably thought he was backing Jesus into a rhetorical corner:

> *"You have answered correctly," Jesus replied. "Do this and you will live."*
>
> *But he wanted to justify himself, so he asked Jesus, "And who is my neighbor?"*
>
> *In reply, Jesus said: "A man was going down from Jerusalem to Jericho, when he was attacked by robbers. They stripped him of his clothes, beat him and went away, leaving him half dead. A priest happened to be going down the same road, and when he saw the man, he passed by on the other side. So too, a Levite, when he came to the place and saw him, passed by on the other side. But a Samaritan, as he traveled, came where the man was; and when he saw him, he took pity on him. He went to him and bandaged his wounds, pouring on oil and wine. Then he put the man on his own donkey,*

brought him to an inn and took care of him. The next day
he took out two denarii [silver coins] and gave them to the
innkeeper. 'Look after him,' he said, 'and when I return, I will
reimburse you for any extra expense you may have.'

"Which of these three do you think was a neighbor to the
man who fell into the hands of robbers?"

The expert in the law replied, "The one who had mercy on
him."

Jesus told him, "Go and do likewise." [196]

"Who is my neighbor?" the man asked. Jesus responded by
telling the story of a man who was not family, who was not a friend,
who was a member of a despised race, someone totally unlike the
expert in the law, even a traditional enemy of the Jews!

In fact, Samaritans were the *last* people a Jew would think of
as "my neighbor." Sure, they lived nearby, but they were a different
race, a different class, a different religion, a different lifestyle, and
they were, every one of them, descended from political traitors and
collaborators.

But Jesus told the story and then asked the Pharisee, "How do
you define 'neighbor' now?"

In reply, the man couldn't even bring himself to say, "The
Samaritan." Instead, he said, "The one who had mercy on him."
Incredibly, deliciously, Jesus managed to give two conventional
answers to a question that was intended to trap him, and then he
got his would-be accuser to say the truly scandalous words.

Author and poet Wendell Berry writes:

We are to love one another, and this love is to be more
comprehensive than our love for family and friends and tribe
and nation. We are to love our neighbors though they may be
strangers to us. We are to love our enemies. And this is to be a
practical love; it is to be practiced, here and now. [197]

"Love God," Jesus said. "Love all." Perhaps part of the reason Jesus mentioned those two commandments together is because "loving God" is not only first in importance, but also first in sequence. That is, I must love God or I will never have the power to love my neighbor as myself. Or, to put it another way, *if* I love God, *then* (and only then) I can love everyone else.

LOVE MUCH

There is one more thing to notice in Jesus' words about the greatest commandment: the importance of the prepositions. He said, "Love the Lord your God *with* all your heart and *with* all your soul and *with* all your mind," and "Love your neighbor *as* yourself."[198] The "with" and the "as" are critical. The "with" is the *means* to accomplish the "as." The "with" supplies the *power* to accomplish the "as." It takes a wholehearted love for God to make me a person who can truly love others as myself, nourishing and cherishing them as I would myself.[199]

On one occasion, Jesus was invited to eat dinner at the house of a Pharisee named Simon. The invitation itself conferred honor on Jesus, but for some reason, when he arrived, he was treated poorly. The usual conventions of hospitality—washing the guest's feet, greeting him with a kiss, and offering fragrant oil for his head— were neglected. But a woman with a bad reputation managed to gain entrance to the place, washed Jesus' feet with her tears, wiped them with her hair, and opened an alabaster jar of precious ointment and poured it on Jesus' feet.

The Pharisee sneered inwardly, thinking, *"If this man were a prophet, he would have known who and what sort of woman this is who is touching him, for she is a sinner."*[200] Jesus interrupted the man's silent thoughts:

> *"Simon, I have something to say to you." And he answered, "Say it, Teacher."*

"A certain moneylender had two debtors. One owed five hundred denarii, and the other fifty. When they could not pay, he cancelled the debt of both. Now which of them will love him more?" Simon answered, "The one, I suppose, for whom he cancelled the larger debt." And he said to him, "You have judged rightly." Then turning toward the woman he said to Simon, "Do you see this woman? I entered your house; you gave me no water for my feet, but she has wet my feet with her tears and wiped them with her hair. You gave me no kiss, but from the time I came in she has not ceased to kiss my feet. You did not anoint my head with oil, but she has anointed my feet with ointment. Therefore I tell you, her sins, which are many, are forgiven—for she loved much. But he who is forgiven little, loves little."[201]

What a contrast in that passage. Jesus' host was a man who obeyed the letter of God's laws to the last detail, but failed in love, both toward Jesus and toward the woman. The woman, however, though her past was apparently sordid, enjoyed forgiveness and blessing from Jesus, "for she loved much."

This is surely the sort of thing Jesus meant when he said your righteousness must exceed the righteousness of the scribes and Pharisees. He did not mean to be even more legalistic than they were; he meant to love like the woman in Simon's house. He meant to love much. He meant to love with heart, soul, mind, and strength. He meant to love *with* and to love *as*. He meant to love God, love all, and love much.

Dallas Willard writes:

Is it then hard to do the things with which Jesus illustrates the kingdom heart of love? . . . It is very hard indeed if you have not been substantially transformed in the depths of your being, in the intricacies of your thoughts, feelings, assurances, and dispositions, in such a way that you are permeated with love. Once that happens, then it is not hard. What would be hard is to act the way you acted before. [202]

THE FINAL WORD

It is the word on which all words hang: *love.* Jesus says to make it the defining characteristic of your relationship with him and with others.

So the final word for this week is to start as the forgiven woman of Luke 7 did. Find a way to break open an alabaster jar at the feet of Jesus. Start with love for him, and pray for it to overflow and permeate your relationships and interactions with all others.

Depending on your personality, that may mean writing a prayer of love and thanks to Jesus. It may involve a worship service experience. It may entail some time listening to the worship songs that most evoke love for God in you. It may provoke a financial offering of some kind, or some other kind of sacrifice. It may be something intensely personal or appropriately public.

Whatever shape it may take, perform an act of "much love" toward God, and pray that it will be only the beginning.

Love God. Love all. Love much.

10

THE WORD THAT SINGS AND DANCES

Maybe it is a function of the 24/7 news cycle. Or it could be that news—bad news, particularly—travels faster and farther than ever before. Or maybe there really is more bad news today, and more reasons to feel sad.

Sure, the twentieth century saw the defeat of Nazism and the collapse of Soviet communism. In the span of just a couple of generations, cures were discovered or developed for polio, measles, typhus, yellow fever, diphtheria, smallpox, and malaria. Infant mortality rates have never been lower. Life expectancy has never been higher.

Yet, worldwide, more people live in slavery than at any time in human history—twenty-seven million, by some estimates.[203] Pornography pervades our society, and its harmful effects are incalculable. Our world reels from global recession, systemic poverty, child abuse, rampant disease, pollution, natural disasters, terrorism, and war. Once-prosperous cities are bedeviled by gang wars, corruption, and bankruptcy. Once-promising futures are ruined by stress, depression, and drug abuse. In the world's most affluent countries, suicide is the leading cause of death among people between the ages of fifteen and forty-nine, claiming more victims than cancer and heart disease.[204]

For all our advancements and attempts at improvement, we still need a word from Jesus. He told his first followers, "While you are in the world, you will have to suffer. But cheer up! I have defeated the world."[205] As he did in the days of murderous Herods and conquering Caesars, he gives to his followers today the word that sings and dances: *rejoice.*

FULLNESS OF JOY

Jesus knew his share of sadness, of course—more than his share, in fact. His life and death were a fulfillment of the prophet's words, "He was despised and rejected—a man of sorrows, acquainted with deepest grief."[206] "He came into the very world he created," the Bible says, "but the world didn't recognize him."[207] "He came to his own people, but they didn't want him."[208] He suffered rejection, temptation, ridicule, criticism, and betrayal—and that was *before* his arrest and crucifixion!

Nonetheless, writes Dallas Willard,

> *Jesus himself was and is a joyous, creative person. . . . One of the most outstanding features of Jesus' personality was precisely an abundance of joy. This he left as an inheritance to his students, "that their joy may be full" (John 15:11). And they did not say, "Pass the aspirin," for he was well known to those around him as a happy man. It is deeply illuminating of kingdom living to understand that his steady happiness was not ruled out by his experience of sorrow and even grief.*[209]

Jesus lived a life of joy, to such an extent that his critics branded him a party animal.[210] The Gospels depict him repeatedly feasting with friends. His stories delighted the crowds. His presence attracted them. On at least one occasion, his intimacy with his Father transported and transfigured him in such a way that his friends hated to see it stop.[211] His life exemplified the truth, "In your presence there is fullness of joy."[212]

Jesus didn't just exhibit fullness of joy. He doesn't just possess fullness of joy. He commands it. He imparts it. He says to you, "Rejoice." He says it knowing of your worries and fears. He says it in full awareness of your problems. He says it, conscious of your limitations and cognizant of the obstacles you face. He says it, not because it is easy, but because it is possible.

Okay, you might say. *But how?*

GIVE YOURSELF PERMISSION TO REJOICE

You may not feel as if you have any right to rejoice. "With all the suffering in the world, who can be happy?" You may have grown up in a family or community that promoted stoicism or cynicism. You may see the glass not only as half empty rather than half full, but also how dirty the glass is, or the ring it leaves on the table. Rejoicing may not come naturally or easily to you at all.

Some people need to give themselves *permission* to rejoice. Whatever anyone else may do, whatever your past has been like, give yourself permission to smile, laugh, and lighten your mood. Resist the temptation to be serious or morose; find something positive and rejoice in it.

In her best-selling book *One Thousand Gifts*, Ann Voskamp tells her story, which for years resembled a Shakespearean tragedy more than a Disney movie. When she was a child, her younger sister chased a cat into a country road and was crushed under the wheels of a delivery truck. Ann's mother, unable to cope with the heartbreak, checked herself into a psychiatric hospital. Ann's father was never the same. A devastating loss like that can scar a person, and it did so to Ann, for a long time. But then one day, challenged by a friend, she resolved to make it her daily task to notice, list, and—in writing—give thanks for the good things she enjoyed each day, no matter how small or routine, and to keep going until she had noticed one thousand gifts. Learning to rejoice in gifts that would otherwise have gone unnoticed and unremarked changed her life (and, through her book and ministry, the lives of many other people as well).

"Joy does not simply happen to us," writes Henri Nouwen. "We have to choose joy and keep choosing it every day."[213] So give yourself permission to choose joy. And find ways to keep choosing it, day after day.

GIVE YOURSELF REASONS TO REJOICE

Songwriter Matt Redman claimed to find "10,000 Reasons" for his heart to sing God's praises. That may be a conservative estimate. If you can give yourself permission to rejoice, you can also heed the word that sings and dances by giving yourself reasons to rejoice. For example:

Rejoice in creation. John Calvin said, "There is not one little blade of grass, there is no color in this world that is not intended to make men rejoice."[214] How many blades of grass are there? Billions? Zillions? That's how many reasons God has given you to rejoice. How many different colors and shades brighten your home, neighborhood, workplace—or even your hospital room? Those are just some of the blessings God has given you, along with the ability to see them. Open your eyes to them. Ann Voskamp writes:

> *You've got to figure out a way to stay awake to your one wild and beautiful life.*
>
> *Moments. This is all we have. Moments. Microscopic, fleeting moments.*
>
> *How many moments of our lives have our eyes been wide-open—but we've been rushing, racing, sleeping right through?*
>
> *How many of the popsicle days and run-and-twirl-and-spin days? How many of the moments of melting ice cream and crazy laughter and dangling bare feet and the sun setting down low, igniting the wonder of now?*
>
> *Someone—wake us up! To the beating of wings and splashing of water, the settling of fog at twilight—the way the leaves and the childhood can slip away in the woods, torched*

with the last of summer.

Do you hear me whispering to you holding these pages? Time's blurring by and everyone's slipping past and how do we wake to the moments? Wake to the joy that really matters?

How do we stop living like life is an emergency— something to be sped wildly through? Life is not an emergency.

How do we start believing that life can be carried only in the hands of the unhurried. . .a bubble held in awe.

How do we stop wolfing this one life down? Because life is our only dessert—too brief, too sweet, too delectable to hurry.

Just to live like a boy I once knew, who paused between bites to wiggle his one loose tooth and smiled, his mouth full of sweet, "I love you, Mom. . .and all this."

All this—all these moments. . .all these are for you. Isn't that the Voice we have to learn to hear? [215]

Rejoice in God. Charles Haddon Spurgeon, known as the "Prince of Preachers," writes, "To rejoice in temporal comforts is dangerous, to rejoice in self is foolish, to rejoice in sin is fatal, but to rejoice in God is heavenly."[216] Rejoice in God. Rejoice in his existence. Rejoice in his presence. Rejoice in his activity in your life. Rejoice in his patience with you. Rejoice in his sovereignty, wisdom, love, and grace. Say with Mary, the mother of Jesus, "How my spirit rejoices in God my Savior!"[217]

Rejoice in your salvation. In the days of his earthly ministry, Jesus once chose seventy people from among the larger group of his followers and sent them out in pairs as an advance team to towns and villages he intended to visit. He empowered them to bless and heal and preach about the kingdom of God. When those seventy completed their mission, "they joyfully reported to him, 'Lord, even the demons obey us when we use your name!' "[218] Jesus acknowledged that he had given them authority over all the works of the evil one. "But," he said, "don't rejoice because evil spirits obey you; rejoice because your names are registered in heaven."[219] The Lord's words underscore what ought to be a cause of overflowing joy in your life, if you have experienced new life in Christ. Rejoice that your name is written in heaven. Rejoice that your name has been entered in the Lamb's Book of Life. Rejoice that you are accepted in Christ.[220] Rejoice at your "redemption through his blood, the forgiveness of sins, in accordance with the riches of God's grace."[221]

Rejoice in your blessings. The Salvation Army's "prophet of holiness," Samuel Logan Brengle, writes:

> *Some years ago a sanctified woman went alone to keep her daily hour with God. But to her surprise, it seemed that she could not find Him, either in prayer or in His Word. She searched her heart for evidence of sin, but the Spirit showed her nothing contrary to God. She searched her memory for any breach of covenant, any broken vows, but could find none.*
>
> *Then she asked the Lord to show her if there were any duty unfulfilled, any command unnoticed, and quick as thought came the often-read words, "Rejoice evermore" (1 Thessalonians 5:16, KJV). "Have you done that this morning?" She had not.*
>
> *At once she began to count her blessings and thank the Lord for each one, and rejoice in Him for all the ways He had led her, and the gifts He had bestowed, and in a very few minutes the Lord stood revealed to her spiritual consciousness.*
>
> *She had not committed sin, nor resisted the Spirit, but she had not turned on the main, and so her soul was not flooded with living waters. But that morning she learned a lifelong lesson, and she has ever since safeguarded her soul by obeying the many commands to "rejoice in the Lord."[222]*

Rejoice with others. It can be a wonderful thing to work alongside others in a meaningful task. Jesus told his first followers, "Do you not say, 'There are yet four months, and then comes the harvest'? Behold, I say to you, lift up your eyes and look on the fields, that they are white for harvest. Already he who reaps is receiving wages and is gathering fruit for life eternal; so that he who sows and he who reaps may rejoice together."[223] Take time to appreciate those who work before, beside, and over you in the church, in your workplace, and in society. Rejoice with those with whom you partner in the church office, nursery, or worship team. Bask in the company of the people God has placed alongside you. Express your appreciation to them. Pray for them and with them. Thank God for placing them close to you.

Rejoice in what God is doing. When Jesus approached Jerusalem on the day we commemorate as Palm Sunday, crowds began to form along the road and hail his approach. The Bible says:

> *The whole crowd of disciples began joyfully to praise God in*
> *loud voices for all the miracles they had seen:*
> *"Blessed is the king who comes in the name of the Lord!"*
>
> *"Peace in heaven and glory in the highest!"* [224]

They rejoiced at what Jesus was doing. They rejoiced at his bold announcement of the kingdom's arrival. They rejoiced to be witnesses of the work of God. You and I can, and should, do the same. Is God moving in your community? In your church? Rejoice! Is he sending new laborers into fields of ministry? Rejoice! Is he moving through you or someone else? Rejoice! Is he convicting, inspiring, transforming, and refining people? Rejoice!

Rejoice in worship. After the traumatic events of his trial, crucifixion, and burial, Jesus rose from the dead and began to appear to his followers in surprising ways and unexpected places. The apostle John records, "When it was evening on that day, the first day of the week, and when the doors were shut where the disciples were, for fear of the Jews, Jesus came and stood in their midst and said to them, 'Peace be with you.' And when He had said this, He showed them both His hands and His side. The disciples then rejoiced when they saw the Lord."[225] The disciples rejoiced when Jesus made himself known to them. They rejoiced when his presence banished their fears, lifted their spirits, and empowered their testimony. What better description could there be of a worship experience in a living church, where Jesus makes himself known, banishes fear, lifts spirits, and empowers the testimony of the saints? So rejoice in worship. Rejoice that you can gather with others to see the Lord. Rejoice when you experience the risen Christ. Rejoice in such moments and encounters with your Lord, whether they happen in church or on your morning commute or in your kitchen at midday.

Rejoice in life celebrations. When Jesus gathered with his closest friends and followers in the upper room before his arrest, he told them, "You've no idea how much I have looked forward to eating this Passover meal with you before I enter my time of suffering."[226] There were certainly many reasons for Jesus to say that, but one possible reason is simply that he reveled in moments of celebration and companionship. So when Jesus gives us the word that sings and dances, we would do well to heed his word by rejoicing in life celebrations: birthdays, anniversaries, holidays, reunions, and more. Join wholeheartedly in the festivals of your faith (Christmas, Easter, etc.). Revel in cultural events (Independence Day, county fairs, etc.). Establish festive family traditions. Create memories for yourself and your loved ones. Devise ways to transform ordinary days and moments into celebrations (like the father who occasionally yanked his kids out of bed a few minutes after bedtime prayers and bundled them into the car in their pajamas for a "mystery ride" to an ice cream stand or stargazing perch).

Rejoice in misfortune. When Jesus tells us to rejoice, he does not limit our reasons for rejoicing to sunny skies and sugary donuts. He tells us to rejoice even in misfortune. He says, "Blessed are you when others revile you and persecute you and utter all kinds of evil against you falsely on my account. Rejoice and be glad."[227] Really? Rejoice when I am reviled? When I am persecuted? When people lie and gossip about me? Yes, Jesus says. And James reinforces the message in his letter to the church: "Dear brothers and sisters, when troubles come your way, consider it an opportunity for great joy. For you know that when your faith is tested, your endurance has a chance to grow. So let it grow, for when your endurance is fully developed, you will be perfect and complete, needing nothing."[228] In other words, rejoice in misfortune because it is making you better—even beautiful. In her book *Death: The Final Stage of Growth*, Elisabeth Kübler-Ross writes, "The most beautiful people we have known are those who have known defeat, known suffering, known struggle, known loss, and have found their way out of the depths. These persons have an appreciation, sensitivity, and an understanding of life that fills them with compassion, gentleness, and a deep loving concern. Beautiful people do not just happen."[229] No, they do not. They are produced by rejoicing through struggle.

Rejoice in your future hope. When Jesus said you are blessed when others revile you, persecute you, and speak meanly and falsely about you for his sake, he went further. He said, "Rejoice and be glad, for your reward is great in heaven, for so they persecuted the prophets who were before you."[230] In other words, rejoice in your future hope and coming reward. Rejoice that this world's suffering—even its benefit—is not the best you can hope for. Rejoice in the knowledge that, for all who have experienced new life in Christ, "the best is yet to be."[231] Rejoice that "whatever we may have to go through now is less than nothing compared with the magnificent future God has planned for us."[232]

GIVE YOURSELF TIME TO REJOICE

Perhaps one of the reasons joy seems to be in such short supply in our day is that time is in such short supply. We are so often pressed and stressed, "anxious and troubled about many things,"[233] that we fail to give ourselves the time necessary to live consciously, purposefully, and attentively—things that would, in turn, help us to live joyfully.

Andrew Murray, in his classic work *Abide in Christ*, writes:

Child of God. . .remember what the Lord says. At the close of the parable of the Vine He adds these precious words: "These things have I spoken unto you, that my joy might abide in you, and that your joy might be full." Claim the joy as part of the branch life—not the first part or the chief part, but as the blessed proof of the sufficiency of Christ to satisfy every need of the soul. Be happy. Cultivate gladness. If there are times when it comes of itself, and the heart feels the unutterable joy of the Saviour's presence, praise God for it, and seek to maintain it. If at other times feelings are dull, and the experience of the joy not such as you could wish it, still praise God for the life of unutterable blessedness to which you have been redeemed. In this, too, the word holds good: "According to your faith be it unto you." As you claim all the other gifts in Jesus, ever claim this one too—not for your own sake, but for His and the Father's glory. "My joy in you"; "that my joy may abide in you"; "my joy fulfilled in themselves"—these are Jesus' own words. It is impossible to take Him wholly and heartily, and not to get His joy too. Therefore, "Rejoice in the Lord always; and again I say, Rejoice."[234]

Joy will not come to you by accident. It will not come in the rush and hustle of a hurried life. It will come only when you slow down or stop in the mad dash of daily life and take time—even a few moments—to breathe. To look up from your smartphone. To reflect. To notice blessings. To smile. To receive a smile. To cultivate gladness. To feel the unutterable joy of the Savior's presence. To "praise God for the life of unutterable blessedness to which you have been redeemed." To rejoice in the Lord.

THE FINAL WORD

Leonard Sweet points out in his book *Soul Salsa*:

> *Jesus came to make all of life a dance. A Gnostic hymn about Jesus picked up this theme in graphic terms:*
>
> *But as for Me, if thou wouldst know what I was:*
> *In a word I am the Word who did dance*
> *All things, and was not shamed at all.*
> *'Twas I who leapt and danced.* [235]

When was the last time you leapt for joy? When was the last time you danced? Laughed out loud? Skipped? Experienced joy?

The last word for this chapter is this: Heed the word that dances and sings by doing whatever it takes to do one or the other in the next twenty-four hours. Dance. Sing. Leap. Laugh out loud.

Will watching a particular sitcom episode do the trick? Whatever it takes.

Is there a favorite song you can't resist singing along to? Whatever it takes.

A friend who always makes you laugh? Whatever it takes.

A YouTube video? A website? A funny hat? Whatever it takes.

"Rejoice in the Lord always. I will say it again: Rejoice!" [236]

THE WORD FOR A DARK WORLD

You've felt it. We all have.

Someone you care about is hurting, Maybe he or she has experienced a setback. A devastating diagnosis. A debilitating grief. Or maybe even a string of such things, one after the other.

There he or she stands before you. Eyes filled with tears. Lip quivering. And there is nothing you can do. You feel utterly powerless.

It's a horrible feeling. You want so badly to say something. Do something. Help somehow. But what? How?

When Jesus walked the earth, his neighbors, friends, and followers may have felt much the same way. Times were tough. Life was hard. Disease was common, poverty widespread. People didn't just struggle to make ends meet; they were lucky to have ends, whether they ever met or not. Whatever parts of their lives the Roman Empire didn't control, the religious authorities did. Their hopes were few. Their aspirations, humble. Their power, nonexistent.

Then into their lives strode Jesus. He knew them. Knew their powerlessness. Knew the boundaries of their narrow, restricted lives, and the outlines of their low expectations. But he knew more than that. He knew what they did not know and saw what they did not see. And he said what they had never heard, never imagined. He spoke into their lives the word for a dark world:

> "You are the light of the world. A town built on a hill cannot
> be hidden. Neither do people light a lamp and put it under
> a bowl. Instead they put it on its stand, and it gives light to
> everyone in the house. In the same way, let your light shine

*before others, that they may see your good deeds and glorify
your Father in heaven."* [237]

Those are familiar words to most church folk. Maybe *too*
familiar. Our familiarity with these words of Jesus may prevent us
from hearing and grasping what he said.

For example, notice what he *didn't* say. He didn't say, "You *can
be* the light of the world." He didn't suggest that we merely have
that potential. He didn't encourage us to *become* the light of the
world.

Neither did he say, "You must *learn* to be the light of the world."
He offered no training programs or how-to hints.

He also didn't say, "You should light your own lamp," advising
us to self-ignite or self-generate the light this world needs.

He said, "You *are* the light of the world." He spoke in the
present tense to his followers. He pronounced it as a fait accompli,
a done deal. He stated it matter-of-factly. Authoritatively. And
conclusively.

You are the light of the world.

SHINE

When Jesus said, "A town built on a hill cannot be hidden," [238]
he may have pointed to the Galilean hill town of Safed (Tzfat).
It is not only visible from great distances (including the hillsides
around Capernaum thought to be the likely sites of Jesus' Sermon
on the Mount), but its nearly three-thousand-foot elevation makes
Safed the highest city in Israel. So when Jesus said, "You are the
light of the world," he may have been comparing his followers to
the light that blazed from the highest point in the land and the
city from which it blazed.

You pierce the darkness. Strike a single match in the utter darkness
of an underground cavern and the tiny light's power will amaze you.

A flickering campfire can be seen from miles away on a moonless night. The light of Proxima Centauri, the closest star to Earth, travels through nearly 25 *trillion* miles of darkness before reaching Earth. Light pierces the darkness. It does not shy from darkness or try to avoid it, as if darkness somehow has the advantage. It is not so offended by the dark that it hides itself. It does not act as if the darkness will somehow soil it or spoil it. It penetrates. It triumphs. It overcomes. Every time.

You provide a guide. Even on the cloudiest night, the light from Safed offered a guide to travelers in the Galilee. Travelers needed only to look at the light on the heights to orient themselves and find the way home. So it is with you. You are a guide to those around you who may be wandering and wondering, far from home. Even those whose names you don't know may be looking to you and your example: *Why does he seem so gracious and kind? How does she persevere through so much affliction? Could I find the way to God by watching them?*

You present a target. When Jesus said, "A city set on a hill cannot be hidden,"[239] he may have referred not only to the visibility of its position, but also to its value as a strategic target. Over the years, the city of Safed has been both a mighty fortress and a military objective. It was occupied by the tribe of Naphtali after the conquest of Canaan and was one of the cities fortified by Josephus during the Jewish wars against Rome. Since then, its tactical value has made it a priority to Crusader, Muslim, Ottoman, Jewish, and Arab armies. Similarly, followers of Jesus will always present a strategic target to those who fear, hate, resent, or misunderstand Jesus and his Gospel. Though no one wants to be a target, Jesus not only warned us but also encouraged us, saying, "Blessed are those who are persecuted for righteousness' sake, for theirs is the kingdom of heaven. Blessed are you when others revile you and persecute you and utter all kinds of evil against you falsely on my account. Rejoice and be glad, for your reward is great in heaven, for so they persecuted the prophets who were before you."[240]

You proclaim good news. The Jerusalem Talmud identifies Safed as one of five high points throughout Galilee and Judea where fires were lit to announce the new moon and religious festivals to Jesus' contemporaries. A massive bonfire was kindled in Jerusalem, signaling watchmen on successive mountaintops throughout the country. The Safed peak is thought to have been the site of the northernmost signal fire, proclaiming to the Jews of the area—and even those living in Syria, the northern cities of the Decapolis, and the Tetrarchy of Philip—the good news of a new month or the commencement of a festival. Like those fires, our lives proclaim good news to those around us who are bound by sin, bowed by pain, and blinded by darkness.

"In the same way," Jesus says, "let your light shine."[241] It is not something we can generate on our own. It is not something we can force. It is not something we must struggle, stress, and strive to do. As the children's chorus says, "This little light of mine, I'm gonna let it shine." Just let it shine.

GET OUT MORE

Though we *are* the light of the world and we need only to "let it shine," as Jesus says, there are still things we can do to enhance the light. One of those things is to get out more. Light travels. It travels fast (nearly 671 million miles an hour). It travels far. It never stays where it starts. It gets out into the darkness around it.

Too often, we who say we follow Jesus don't do what Jesus did. When we are faced with someone whose life is messy, whose beliefs are confused, and whose language or lifestyle is rough, we tend to get offended. Even appalled. And then we either say or do something judgmental or find the quickest off-ramp in the relationship (or both).

But light isn't offended by darkness. It doesn't retreat from darkness. It just keeps getting out there. It keeps shining, wherever it is. And Jesus says we are light, just like he is. (He not only said, "You are the light of the world," but also "I am the light of the world").[242] He wants us to risk our reputation, as he did. He wants us to earn criticism from religious folk. He wants us to eat and drink with "tax collectors" and "sinners." He wants us to get out of our tidy Christian ghettos and, rather than spending every spare moment in church activities, find time to hang out with people who are far from God. Not to judge them. Not to demand some Christian standard of behavior from them. Not to look down our noses at them or use them as object lessons or sermon illustrations, but to truly and genuinely be their friends, accepting them, relating to them, expressing interest in what they think and what they enjoy, and not trying to squeeze them into our mold.

As *The Message* says, paraphrasing Jesus' words, "Shine! Keep open house; be generous with your lives. By opening up to others, you'll prompt people to open up with God, this generous Father in heaven."[243]

BE WHO YOU ARE, WHERE YOU ARE

Randy Harris, in his book *Living Jesus*, tells of his regular meetings with "a group of honors ministry students who intend to make a difference in the world."[244] He relates the group's discussions concerning the Sermon on the Mount, in which Jesus called us "the light of the world," then says:

> *Finally, a student concluded the discussion this way: "One thing I've noticed is that if you really are going to start living this way and you start making big changes in your life, eventually it starts to change who you are from the inside. The more you live the teachings out, the more it becomes natural*

*to you—it's who you are. And once you get there, you end
up living a life that creates peace among everyone you are
around.* [245]

In other words, "let *your* light shine." Not someone else's. Not the pastor's. Yours.

God gave you a unique personality, background, and experience for a reason. He didn't intend to shine through a poor copy of someone else; he wants you to be *you*, so *your* light can shine. Don't try to fake it. Don't try to be someone else. Don't don a Christian "persona." Just be who you are, where you are.

Don't hold back, either. Don't be afraid to talk openly about your life, your church, your relationship with God. Don't hesitate to offer to pray with someone or refer to things you're learning or enjoying through worship, prayer, and Bible study—not in "churchspeak" (the vocabulary, accent, or tone that some of us adopt after we've been around the church or other Christians for a while; jargon that sounds weird or confusing to people outside the church), but in normal, everyday speech. As the widely known Internet meme says, "Be yourself; everyone else is already taken."

DO GOOD

Notice also that Jesus said, "Let your light shine before others, that they may see your good deeds and glorify your Father in heaven." [246] Good deeds are not the light; *you* are the light. But as you pierce the darkness, provide a guide, present a target, and proclaim good news, people will notice the fruit of your life. They will see your good deeds.

This is not a contradiction to Jesus' words in Matthew 6:1, where he says, "Beware of doing your good deeds conspicuously to catch men's eyes or you will miss the reward of your Heavenly Father." [247] You should not do good things to be seen, but you should always be seen doing good things.

John Gill, in his exposition of the entire Bible, explains what Jesus means by "good deeds":

> *Meaning their zeal and fervency; their plainness and*
> *openness; their sincerity, faithfulness, and integrity; their*
> *courage and intrepidity; their diligence, industry, and*
> *indefatigableness in preaching the Gospel; their strict regard to*
> *truth, the honour of Christ, and the good of souls; as also their*
> *very great care and concern to recommend the doctrines of*
> *grace, by their example in their lives and conversations.* [248]

As followers of Jesus, who is "the Light of the world," we should let our lights shine as he did. "He went about doing good,"[249] and so should we. Like responsible backwoods campers, who always leave the trail and campsite better than they found it, we must do all we can to leave every place and everyone better than we found them, by our zeal and fervency, plainness and openness, our sincerity, faithfulness, and integrity; our courage and intrepidity; our diligence, industry, and indefatigableness in preaching the Gospel; our strict regard to truth, the honor of Christ, the good of souls, and our care and concern to recommend the doctrines of grace, by our example in our lives and conversation.

GIVE GLORY TO GOD

Anyone who has worked as a server in a restaurant can testify that no one wants to work the Sunday dinner shift. The following letter explains why:

> *I am both a Christian and a Server at a downtown Nashville*
> *restaurant. One of the most personally embarrassing ordeals*
> *I ever go through at work is when there is a large, highly*

publicized Christian event, and "my people" come out en masse to eat. Only because I walked into the break-room during a gripe session and found her in mid-sentence, a fellow server asked me an honest and long-deserved question, "Why are religious people the worst tippers?"

It's true. As a whole, Christians are thought of by restaurant workers to be among the absolute worst tippers of any single identifiable group. Sundays after church, and during events like the one mentioned, Christians go out in large numbers, perhaps unaware of how poorly they are representing the gospel to a very specific and largely "unreached" people group—their servers. . . .

Most of the time. . .the typical Christian comes across as downright stingy. Don't believe me? Ask any server's honest opinion (when they're not waiting on you, of course).

Tonight, a Christian couple had a problem with their food taking much longer than it should have (remember, they were on their way to the concert). Management was diligent to attempt to rectify the problem by giving the couple half off their meal (a $20 discount where I work). Guess what they left the server? Thirty cents—then they rushed out the door to go worship God! (Matt. 5:23–4). Of course he let me know about that! As someone with whom I've had many conversations about the gospel, and a genuinely open person ordinarily, he could only rant, and ask me, "Do unto others, huh? Turn the other cheek, huh? What about forgiveness?! Or patience??? And these are the people that dress up every Sunday and give their ten percent, and think that earns them the right to go to heaven?" (I'm not exaggerating—that is exactly what he said, except for the parts not suitable for print.) If only that were an isolated incident!

We fail to realize that because we tend to appear all at

once, in large groups, giving good service becomes extremely difficult. Servers frequently wind up penalized rather than blessed by our presence, and then we "judge" them under extreme conditions. The server mentioned earlier? She was upset because her customers not only left her a poor tip; to make matters immeasurably worse, they also left her a gospel tract. This is too common an occurrence. [250]

This ought not to be so. Jesus said, "Let your light shine before others, that they may see your good deeds and glorify your Father in heaven." [251] The apostle Peter writes, "Live such good lives among the pagans that, though they accuse you of doing wrong, they may see your good deeds and glorify God on the day he visits us." [252] The "red letter life" does not embarrass God; it glorifies him. Because you "shine before others," you must "be wise in the way you act toward outsiders; make the most of every opportunity," [253] and "be generous on every occasion." [254]

You don't have to go around saying, "Praise the Lord," and "Glory to God." You can trust those who are watching your life to make their own application. You may be a target, and they may be reluctant to give glory to God, but "wisdom is shown to be right by the lives of those who follow it." [255] Let your life show the wisdom of the Gospel. Let your actions encourage glory to God, even from those who are far from him.

THE FINAL WORD

This chapter's "final word" is simple: Find a candle. Surely you have one somewhere in your house. If not, purchase one on your next trip to the store.

Light it and place it somewhere prominent, somewhere you will see it often throughout the next twenty-four hours. Let it remind you, each time you see it, that "you are the light of the world." Let it prompt you to "let your light shine." Let it shape your awareness and your actions "so that [others] may see your good works and give glory to your Father who is in heaven."[256]

THE WORD OF WARNING

The future can be scary.

Sometimes we fear the things we know are coming, like the first drop of a roller coaster or the clap of thunder after a flash of lightning. But most often we fear the future because it is unknown. *Will I flunk algebra? Is she going to break up with me? Are they going to offer me the position? Can I make the rent payment this month? Am I going to lose my job? Are my kids' friends going to lead them astray? What if the test results are positive?* And more.

We fear the unknown because. . .well, because it is unknown. We worry about the future because it is largely out of our control. Sure, we can anticipate some things, and prepare for them, but we can't know everything. We can't plan for every contingency.

Wouldn't it be nice if there were someone in our lives who did know the future? A friend who could see into the unknown? Wouldn't it be nice for someone like that to give us a few tips, some helpful words, to prepare us ahead of time?

Yes, of course it would. And we have such a friend in Jesus. And from his depth of knowledge and breadth of wisdom, he has given us the word that warns: *beware.*

WWJW? (WHAT WOULD JESUS WARN?)

We've become accustomed to warnings in our daily lives. Those of us who live in the city hear car alarms so frequently that they eventually fail to pierce our consciousness. We pass by Caution signs so often that we tend to stop noticing them. Wet Floor, Wet Paint, and Watch Your Head signs may be so familiar that we scarcely see them. And speed limit signs are generally invisible to us unless we see a lighted sign that flashes our actual speed as we approach.

But when Jesus issues a warning, we should pay attention. . .and never stop paying attention. When he says, "Beware," we must not only hear but also heed what he says—especially because he used that word of warning so judiciously and, at times, unexpectedly.

Think about it for a moment. From what you already know of Jesus and the world, what warnings might you expect him to issue? When Jesus says, "Beware," what would you guess his next words to be?

Would you expect him to say, "Beware of sinners, lest they drag you into their folly"? Or "Beware of worldly governments, for they will oppress and enslave you"? Or perhaps "Beware of strong drink"? Or "Beware of loud music"? Or "Beware of zombies, robots, and vampires"? Maybe.

Of course, those last few are not serious. Still, it is surprising that Jesus said none of those things. In fact, of the ten times the Gospels record Jesus using the word *beware* (Greek, *proseko*), he is focusing on just a few things. And it's not too much of a stretch to suppose that his warnings may be just as sound today as they were to his first followers two thousand years ago. Certainly no harm— and perhaps much blessing—can come from heeding his word of warning in our lives today.

BEWARE OF PEOPLE

The broadest warning Jesus could have issued appears in Matthew's Gospel, where Jesus, upon commissioning his twelve closest followers, warns them:

> *"Behold, I am sending you out as sheep in the midst of wolves,*
> *so be wise as serpents and innocent as doves. Beware of*
> *men, for they will deliver you over to courts and flog you in*
> *their synagogues, and you will be dragged before governors*

and kings for my sake, to bear witness before them and the
Gentiles. When they deliver you over, do not be anxious how
you are to speak or what you are to say, for what you are to say
will be given to you in that hour. For it is not you who speak,
but the Spirit of your Father speaking through you. Brother
will deliver brother over to death, and the father his child, and
children will rise against parents and have them put to death,
and you will be hated by all for my name's sake. But the one
who endures to the end will be saved. When they persecute you
in one town, flee to the next, for truly, I say to you, you will
not have gone through all the towns of Israel before the Son of
Man comes." [257]

What an interesting ordination service! Jesus sugarcoats
nothing. He tells his followers, in no uncertain terms, what they
can expect. Like M giving an assignment to James Bond, he warns
them, "Trust no one." In fact, his words are strikingly specific
and comprehensive. He tells them to beware of the state ("They
will deliver you over to courts. . .and you will be dragged before
governors and kings"). He says to beware of religious authorities
("They will. . .flog you in their synagogues"). He even commands
them to beware of family members ("Brother will deliver brother
over to death, and the father his child, and children will rise
against parents and have them put to death"). He makes it clear
that they can be certain of no one ("You will be hated by all for
my name's sake").

Seems harsh, doesn't it? Surely Jesus didn't mean to "beware
of *everyone*," did he? Actually, it seems he did, for John's Gospel
describes Jesus in these words:

Because of the miraculous signs Jesus did in Jerusalem at the
Passover celebration, many began to trust in him. But Jesus

didn't trust them, because he knew human nature. No one needed to tell him what mankind is really like. [258]

In telling his followers to "beware of pretty much everyone," Jesus prescribes the same approach he himself took toward other people, an attitude rooted in his awareness and understanding of the universal sinfulness of human nature, but simultaneously characterized by wisdom and innocence ("wise as serpents and innocent as doves").

BEWARE OF SELF-RIGHTEOUS PEOPLE

Because the four Gospels (Matthew, Mark, Luke, and John) recount some of the same events and words, it is hard to say exactly how many times Jesus warned his followers against self-righteous people. But a quick reading of the following passages will drive home his concerns:

When the Pharisees heard that Jesus had arrived, they came and started to argue with him. Testing him, they demanded that he show them a miraculous sign from heaven to prove his authority.

When he heard this, he sighed deeply in his spirit and said, "Why do these people keep demanding a miraculous sign? I tell you the truth, I will not give this generation any such sign." So he got back into the boat and left them, and he crossed to the other side of the lake.

But the disciples had forgotten to bring any food. They had only one loaf of bread with them in the boat. As they were crossing the lake, Jesus warned them, "Watch out! Beware of the yeast of the Pharisees and of Herod." [259]

Jesus also taught: "Beware of these teachers of religious law! For they like to parade around in flowing robes and receive respectful greetings as they walk in the marketplaces. And how they love the seats of honor in the synagogues and the head table at banquets. Yet they shamelessly cheat widows out of their property and then pretend to be pious by making long prayers in public. Because of this, they will be more severely punished."[260]

> *Meanwhile, the crowds grew until thousands were milling about and stepping on each other. Jesus turned first to his disciples and warned them, "Beware of the yeast of the Pharisees—their hypocrisy. The time is coming when everything that is covered up will be revealed, and all that is secret will be made known to all. Whatever you have said in the dark will be heard in the light, and what you have whispered behind closed doors will be shouted from the housetops for all to hear!"[261]*

Jesus clearly had a problem with Pharisees. He repeatedly warned his earliest followers about them. But here's the interesting thing: The Pharisees had long been "the good guys" in Jewish society and culture. They had preserved the scriptures and reassembled the pieces of Judaism after the Babylonian captivity. They were the "good, churchgoing folks" of their day. They "didn't smoke, didn't chew, didn't go around with girls who do." They were Bible-reading, Bible-believing, and Bible-obeying people. They even produced some mighty fine people who would later become important in the early church—people such as Nicodemus, Joseph of Arimathea, and Saul of Tarsus (later Paul the apostle).

For all that, however, Jesus told his followers to watch out for them. In fact, his warnings against the "leaven" (corrupting influence) of the Pharisees outnumber all his other uses of the word *beware* by almost three to one. Why? I can think of three reasons.

The Pharisees were *arrogant*. Jesus once told a story of a Pharisee and a tax collector who went to pray in the temple at the same time. The tax collector bowed his head and humbly begged for mercy; the Pharisee cocked his head and thanked God that he was nothing like the tax collector.

They were *judgmental*. They were scorekeepers. They set standards of behavior that no one could keep and then condemned others for not measuring up—a stark contrast to the way of Jesus as Larry Osborne pointed out in his book, *Accidental Pharisees*.

> *When it comes to bruised reeds, smoldering wicks, and the weary saints, Pharisees have no patience. They pile on heavy burdens and lots of guilt. But they don't lift a finger to make anything easier. They thin the herd at every opportunity.*
>
> *Not so with Jesus.*
>
> *The bruised reed he will not break. The smoldering wick he will not snuff out. To the weary and heavily burdened he offers rest, a light load, and an easy yoke.* [262]

They were also *hypocritical*. As Jesus said, they presented themselves to others as the picture of righteousness, but they cheated widows—the lowest kind of behavior people could imagine in Jesus' day. They guarded their reputation as keepers and teachers of God's law, but then they made up loopholes to enrich themselves. [263] They attended to their outward appearance as "separated ones" (the probable meaning of the word *Pharisee*), but according to Jesus, they were unclean and corrupt on the inside. [264]

Many people today are spiritual heirs to the Pharisees: arrogant, judgmental, and hypocritical. Unfortunately, some of those folks are faithful churchgoers. Some are leaders in the church. Not all, of course. But enough to make Jesus' words of warning thoroughly relevant and contemporary: Beware of people like that.

BEWARE OF YOUR OWN SELF-RIGHTEOUSNESS

Having warned his followers about the self-righteousness and hypocrisy of the Pharisees, Jesus turns the spotlight on his followers:

> *"Be careful not to practice your righteousness in front of others to be seen by them. If you do, you will have no reward from your Father in heaven.*
>
> *"So when you give to the needy, do not announce it with trumpets, as the hypocrites do in the synagogues and on the streets, to be honored by others. Truly I tell you, they have received their reward in full. But when you give to the needy, do not let your left hand know what your right hand is doing, so that your giving may be in secret. Then your Father, who sees what is done in secret, will reward you.*
>
> *"And when you pray, do not be like the hypocrites, for they love to pray standing in the synagogues and on the street corners to be seen by others. Truly I tell you, they have received their reward in full. But when you pray, go into your room, close the door and pray to your Father, who is unseen. Then your Father, who sees what is done in secret, will reward you. And when you pray, do not keep on babbling like pagans, for they think they will be heard because of their many words. Do not be like them, for your Father knows what you need before you ask him."* [265]

The tricky thing about self-righteousness is that it is extremely difficult to self-diagnose. So Jesus helps us. He warns us to beware of self-righteousness, not only in others, but also in ourselves. He tells us to beware of religious displays. Of announcing our generosity. Of posturing in prayer. In other words, "Don't be Pharisees." Don't give in to the pharisaical tendency to draw attention to yourself and heap honors on yourself.

There is another facet to such self-righteousness, and that is the tendency to compare ourselves to others in ways that puff us up and make others suffer by comparison. Pastor Larry Osborne tells a revealing story:

I remember once meeting with a group of guys who were passionate about their walk with God. Somehow the conversation turned toward people in the church who were not so passionate. Next thing I knew, they were ripping on the way everyone else raised their kids, spent their money, read their Bible, and set their priorities.

It was one of those "aren't you glad we're not like those guys?" conversations.

Now, these were quality men. They were indeed doing a far better job than most in raising their kids, spending their money, reading their Bible, and setting their priorities. The problem wasn't that they noticed it. The problem was what they did with the information. They used it to justify looking down on everyone else. They became arrogant.

When I called them on it, they were mildly remorseful. Sort of like they'd gotten busted for a speeding ticket. But it was clear that no one felt particularly convicted or was determined not to go there again. So I decided to take them on a little journey through Scripture to see God's perspective on the conversation we'd just had.

We started with Satan's prideful fall and moved on from there. But the shocker for most of them was a list of things God hates. It's found in Proverbs 6:16–19. Right at the top of his "I hate it when you do that" list is "haughty eyes," the disgusted and disdainful look of arrogance that parallels the harsh conversation we'd just had.

There are a lot of things that can anger God. Few people

would guess that looking down on others would be at the top
of the list. Yet it is.. . .

   Spiritual arrogance is not a back-of-the-line sin; it's a
front-of-the-line sin. So much so that sometimes I think of it
as an occupational hazard of zealous faith, serious discipleship,
and biblical scholarship. [266]

Ouch. No wonder Jesus warns us (in the Sermon on the
Mount) against our own self-righteousness and spiritual arrogance.
Our attitude, of course, must always be that of Jesus:

Don't push your way to the front; don't sweet-talk your way to
the top. Put yourself aside, and help others get ahead. Don't be
obsessed with getting your own advantage. Forget yourselves
long enough to lend a helping hand. [267]

BEWARE OF GREED

Jesus' next word of warning is similar to his caution about self-
righteousness. Luke, who could be called the first Christian
historian, writes:

Someone in the crowd said to [Jesus], "Teacher, tell my brother
to divide the family inheritance with me." But He said to him,
"Man, who appointed Me a judge or arbitrator over you?"
Then He said to them, "Beware, and be on your guard against
every form of greed; for not even when one has an abundance
does his life consist of his possessions." [268]

At first glance, Jesus' words to the guy in the crowd seem harsh.
Extreme, even. "Who made me the boss of you—and your brother?"
But, as he did on other occasions, [269] Jesus declined to let people
draw him into their family squabbles, and particularly a dispute

that seemed motivated by greed.

More to the point, Jesus uses the man's request as an occasion to warn his followers against greed—a sneaky, stubborn, and corrosive influence. And notice also that Jesus warns against "every form" of greed. How many forms are there?

The guy in the crowd seemed to be a prisoner of the "I want what's coming to me" variety. But there are other types of greed as well. There is the "I want what *you* have" version. And the "I want more than my parents had" kind, as well as the "I want just a little bit more than I have" and "I want just a little more than *he* has" types of greed. In fact, there may be as many kinds of greed as there are kinds of people. So Jesus says to us, "Beware, and be on your guard against every form of greed." Because, he says, "life is not measured by how much you own."[270] Greed does not enrich; it impoverishes. It will not bring contentment; it prevents it. It will always cheat you and leave you poorer than before.

BEWARE OF FALSE PROPHETS

The last warning of Jesus appears just once in the Gospels:

> *"Beware of false prophets who come disguised as harmless sheep but are really vicious wolves. You can identify them by their fruit, that is, by the way they act. Can you pick grapes from thornbushes, or figs from thistles? A good tree produces good fruit, and a bad tree produces bad fruit. A good tree can't produce bad fruit, and a bad tree can't produce good fruit. So every tree that does not produce good fruit is chopped down and thrown into the fire. Yes, just as you can identify a tree by its fruit, so you can identify people by their actions."* [271]

As Bible scholar William Barclay explains, the *Didache*, the "first order book of the Christian Church," which dates to about

AD 100, offered early Christians specific and detailed guidelines about false prophets:

> *A true prophet was to be held in the highest honour; he was to be welcomed; his word must never be disregarded, and his freedom must never be curtailed; but "He shall remain one day, and, if necessary, another day also; but if he remain three days, he is a false prophet." He must never ask for anything but bread. "If he asks for money, he is a false prophet." Prophets all claim to speak in the Spirit, but there is one acid test: "By their characters a true and a false prophet shall be known." "Every prophet that teacheth the truth, if he do not what he teacheth, is a false prophet." If a prophet, claiming to speak in the Spirit, orders a table and a meal to be set before him he is a false prophet. "Whosoever shall say in the Spirit: Give me money or any other things, ye shall not hear him; but if he tell you to give in the matter of others who have need, let no one judge him." If a wanderer comes to a congregation, and wishes to settle there, if he has a trade, "let him work and eat." If he has no trade, "consider in your wisdom how he may not live with you as a Christian in idleness. But if he will not do this, he is a trafficker in Christ. Beware of such."* [272]

In the eyes of the early church, false prophets were people who took advantage of hospitality, asked for money, failed to live up to their own teachings, and expected others to enrich them. Perhaps those things don't quite translate into our twenty-first-century church culture; or maybe they do. "You can identify them by their fruit,"[273] Jesus said, and it is so even today. Beware of those who enrich themselves rather than practice self-denial and self-sacrifice. Beware of those who ask for money. Beware of those who fail to live up to their own teachings. And beware of those who expect to be served, rather than serving others.

THE FINAL WORD

Of all the things Jesus could have warned us about as dangerous to our faith, he chose five: human nature, self-righteousness (our own and others'), greed, and false prophets. Perhaps because they were timely and urgent in his time. Perhaps because they are important in any time.

So the final word is this: Ask Jesus to impress the word *beware* on your mind and heart this week, so that any time you pass a warning light or caution signal, you remember to beware—not only of other people, self-righteous people and false prophets in particular, but also of your own self-righteous tendencies and your own inclination toward covetousness and greed. Let every stoplight, Wet Floor sign, or orange cone on the roadway remind you of the word that warns: *Beware.*

THE WORD OF ABUNDANCE

There are two seas in the land of Jesus.

One is a scene of beauty, a center of commerce whose shores and depths teem with life. Fish abound in its waters. Slopes carpeted with grass encircle this sea. The surrounding countryside is a patchwork of noisy villages and valuable farmland.

The other sea boasts none of those characteristics. Its shores are barren, the atmosphere is harsh, and its bitter waters can neither sustain life nor quench thirst.

The difference is in their *giving*.

The Sea of Galilee sparkles with freshness because it not only receives the water that flows down from the northern mountains, but also gives itself to the winding Jordan River as it flows to the south.

The Dead Sea, on the other hand, receives fresh water daily from the Jordan River, but it keeps it—there is no outflow. All the minerals that wash in from the north become trapped within its boundaries.

The same principle of life and death applies to people. Andrew Murray writes:

> *Wherever there is life, there is a continual interchange*
> *of taking in and giving out, receiving and restoring. The*
> *nourishment I take is given out again in the work I do; the*
> *impressions I receive, in the thoughts and feelings I express.*
> *The one depends on the other—the giving out ever increases*
> *the power of taking in. In the healthy exercise of giving and*
> *taking is all the enjoyment of life.*

It is so in the spiritual life too. There are Christians who look on its blessedness as consisting all in the privilege of ever receiving; they know not how the capacity for receiving is only kept up and enlarged by continual giving up and giving out—how it is only in the emptiness that comes from the parting with what we have, that the divine fullness can flow in. It was a truth our Saviour continually insisted on. [274]

Murray is right. Among Jesus' most oft-spoken words is the word of abundance: *give.*

PRODUCTS AND PROPHETS

Jesus said it repeatedly and emphatically:

"Give to the needy." [275]
"Give without pay." [276]
"Give to the poor." [277]
"Give to everyone who begs from you." [278]
"Give, and it will be given to you." [279]
"Give as freely as you have received!" [280]

Jesus assumes that giving will be a part of his followers' lives. He says:

"*When* you give to the needy." [281]
"*When* you give a dinner or a banquet." [282]
"*When* you give a feast." [283]

Not *if,* but *when.*

Jesus saw things that we don't see. He knew something that we don't know. He understood that "there is more happiness in giving than in receiving." [284] He originated what Henri Nouwen later discovered for himself:

> *Although it often seems that people give only to receive, I*
> *believe that, beyond all our desires to be appreciated, rewarded*
> *and acknowledged, there lies a simple and pure desire to*
> *give. . . . Our humanity comes to its fullest bloom in giving.*
> *We become beautiful people when we give whatever we can*
> *give: a smile, a handshake, a kiss, an embrace, a word of love,*
> *a present, a part of our life. . .all of our life.* [285]

In fact, it may be no coincidence that Jesus' earthly life, from the start—and even before, actually—reflected this truth. We see it on display in the Nativity accounts in Matthew and Luke, the two Gospels that record events surrounding the birth of Jesus. Luke the historian writes:

> *In those days Caesar Augustus issued a decree that a census*
> *should be taken of the entire Roman world. (This was the first*
> *census that took place while Quirinius was governor of Syria.)*
> *And everyone went to their own town to register.*
> *So Joseph also went up from the town of Nazareth in*
> *Galilee to Judea, to Bethlehem the town of David, because*
> *he belonged to the house and line of David. He went there to*
> *register with Mary, who was pledged to be married to him and*
> *was expecting a child. While they were there, the time came for*
> *the baby to be born, and she gave birth to her firstborn, a son.*
> *She wrapped him in cloths and placed him in a manger, because*
> *there was no guest room available for them.* [286]

The story continues with the appearance of a bunch of angels to a group of shepherds somewhere in that vicinity, and the shepherds eventually paying a visit to the newborn Jesus and his parents. We celebrate this event every Christmas, and when we think of giving at Christmas, we usually think of the visit of the magi, which is reported in Matthew's Gospel.

But the magi weren't the only ones who gave something that first Christmas. In fact, it could be argued that there were others who gave more—others whom we would do well to emulate, regardless of whether our culture understands or makes it easy to do so. We tend to be *products of* our culture, instead of being *prophets to* our culture.

Given that you are reading this book, it's likely that you are among the wealthiest, most favored people on the planet. Even in tough economic times, you are among the privileged souls on this planet who had enough to eat yesterday, who had a roof overhead last night, who have constant access to clean water to drink, and who enjoy electricity in their home and shoes on their feet. And more.

Not that there are no needs in your family, your church, or your community. There are. You may be struggling to put food on the table. Or at least to pay all your bills. But still, compared to billions of others in this world, you live comfortably, even richly. And yet, like most of us, you probably still tend to obsess over the things you want, the things you don't have, the things you are hoping, planning, and saving to possess.

You may know that *things* don't bring happiness; but like most of us, you find it hard not to spend as if they do. You may believe that more and more stuff is not what your kids need, but you may often act as if it is. You may agree that spending money, wanting things, and focusing on "stuff" is a reflection of our consumer culture rather than the words and life of Jesus. You may understand that your humanity comes to its fullest bloom in giving, but you're not sure how to nurture its growth.

It's not that hard. It's not a heavy burden. But it is countercultural and counterintuitive. And it has the potential of making you more of a prophet than a product of your culture, if you prayerfully and conscientiously follow the examples that can be found in the Nativity of Jesus.

GIVE HOSPITALITY

Pity the poor innkeeper. He has gotten more bad press over the years than child actors. He's not even mentioned in the Gospel account, but his presence has long been inferred from Luke 2:7, which says, "She wrapped him in cloths and placed him in a manger, because there was no guest room available for them."[287] So, year after year, preachers, poets, and writers have made this businessman into a bad guy, a Scrooge who wouldn't even give the Son of God a room!

But the Bible doesn't say, "She placed him in a manger because the innkeeper wouldn't let them in." It says "there was no room." But at some point—maybe Joseph asked, maybe the innkeeper offered, or maybe they both knew that lodging with the livestock was a common option when the inn filled up—they bedded down with the animals.

In any case, the innkeeper didn't *have* to extend hospitality to them. How was he supposed to know who Jesus was? It's not as if Jesus was wearing a onesie that said "Son of God" on it.

The innkeeper gave the gift of hospitality, probably the best accommodations he had available, to the Holy Family on that first Christmas. It was probably part of God's plan for Jesus to be born in a stable and for perhaps the first Christmas gift of all time to be the gift of hospitality—a Bethlehem businessman offering warmth and shelter to the King of kings.

Hospitality is a gift the church needs to rediscover. It is actually a biblical command: "Practice hospitality,"[288] and "Be quick to give a meal to the hungry, a bed to the homeless."[289] It was a bedrock value among the patriarchs and prophets, and one of the earliest requirements for leadership in the church.[290] It is also a way of giving that fits any income level or standard of living.

Invite someone to church. Host someone in your home. Include someone in your family's holiday and day-to-day gatherings.

Some years ago, my family had the blessing of hosting an international student from West Africa at our Christmas gathering. He was far from home and someone in our church had mentioned to me that this young man expected to be alone over the holidays. So we invited him and included him in our family's celebrations.

It didn't quite turn out like I'd hoped.

He joined us for our Christmas meal. . .which, as usual, would have been sufficient to feed a small country. We also included him in our gift giving, but his eyes nonetheless grew wide and his neck must have gotten sore as he watched the overabundance of gifts being passed around the room.

I was embarrassed. I saw with new eyes how extravagant our celebration was. I caught a glimpse of our wealth. And gluttony. And greed. Rather than our blessing him with our hospitality, we received a much greater gift from him: *perspective*. We were humbled, convicted, and changed.

We still eat too much and spend too much as a family, but we've made it our goal every year to top the previous year's efforts in giving to those outside our family. It has been a tremendous blessing, and it came out of a tiny effort to show hospitality.

It may be a neighbor, a family member, a traveler, an elderly person, or just someone with whom you want to drink coffee. But whatever it is, it will bless you, whether or not it blesses others. So give hospitality. . .like the innkeeper.

GIVE AVAILABILITY

When our first child was born, my wife and I weren't anxious to share that moment with the world. We were asked if a cadre of medical residents could observe my wife's labor. We said no.

After our daughter arrived, we kept the door shut and soaked up our private time, just the three of us, for most of that short hospital stay.

But not Mary and Joseph.

After Jesus was born and placed in a crude manger, Luke records, angels announced the birth to a smelly bunch of shepherds in the hills nearby. The shepherds then "hurried off and found Mary and Joseph, and the baby, who was lying in the manger."[291]

That stable near the inn was probably a lot more public than a small-town hospital's labor and delivery room, but still, who wants shepherds in the birthing room? Not only that, but there's every possibility that Mary and Joseph weren't the only travelers seeking shelter there that night. It may have been a far more communal living situation than our artwork and manger scenes depict.

But in any case, Luke's account makes it apparent that the shepherds were well received by Mary and Joseph. They left rejoicing and spreading the news around the countryside. In fact, for all we know, the shepherds' big mouths may have prompted *other* Bethlehemites to check out the stable scene. Other visitors aren't recorded, but it's possible.

Nonetheless, it seems apparent that Mary and Joseph gave the gift of availability that first Christmas. They opened their hearts, they made time in their schedule, they may even have stayed up later than they'd planned (or liked), answering questions, telling the story, and generally just being there for the people around them.

Judging from the rest of the Gospel accounts, Jesus followed in Mary and Joseph's footsteps. He was constantly making himself available. Sure, he retreated to private places when necessary, but he also gave the gift of availability to Pharisees such as Nicodemus and Simon, as well as sinners, tax collectors, Roman soldiers, and a Canaanite woman.

Author Robert Wicks writes:

Availability is a simple but great gift. The freedom to be present when needed is something special. . . .

Recently when I was in Ireland, I became lost while traveling the back roads near the small west coast town of Corafinne. When I stopped alongside the road to ask directions of a gentleman working there, the brief stop turned into a lovely fifteen minute encounter. I not only received directions but I also found that we wound up talking about a myriad of things.

As I drove away, I thought, "Wasn't it nice that he took out time to talk to me." As I drove a bit farther it finally dawned on me what really had occurred. He hadn't taken out time from his day to be with me; he had made me part of his life.

This kind of attitude is at the heart of a life that reflects an appreciation of the gift of availability. [292]

So try it. Give the gift of availability. To a traveler, perhaps. Or a child or parent. A coworker. Someone who needs a listening ear.

By simply making yourself available, you may open the door to the miraculous. You may actually pave the way for help or healing. Your gift of availability may accomplish far more than you can imagine or dream.

GIVE FREELY

Everyone knows that the magi (or "wise men" as they are traditionally called) gave gifts that first Christmas. Many people who have never read Matthew's account can name the gifts the magi brought to the newborn Jesus:

Jesus was born in Bethlehem, in Judea, in the days when Herod was king of the province. Not long after his birth there arrived from the east a party of astrologers making for Jerusalem and enquiring as they went, "Where is the child born to be king of the Jews? For we saw his star in the east and we have come here to pay homage to him." [293]

After meeting privately with King Herod,

The wise men. . .then went on their way to Bethlehem. And now the star, which they had seen in the east, went in front of them as they travelled until at last it shone immediately above the place where the little child lay. The sight of the star filled them with indescribable joy.

So they went into the house and saw the little child with his mother Mary. And they fell on their knees and worshipped him. Then they opened their treasures and presented him with gifts—gold, incense and myrrh. Then, since they were warned in a dream not to return to Herod, they went back to their own country by a different route. [294]

As familiar as this account is to many people, few ever reflect on the astounding nature of what those foreign dignitaries did. They didn't have to undertake an arduous journey. They weren't required to offer expensive gifts. No one would have noticed if they had stayed home and used their money to buy the latest smartphone.

But they gave nonetheless. They gave willingly. They gave generously. They gave freely.

That kind of giving apparently not only characterized Jesus' life but was a passion of his. He didn't just say, "Give." He said, "Give much."[295] "Give free of charge."[296] "Give to everyone who begs from you."[297] "Give as freely as you have received!"[298] He even suggested giving anonymously.[299] And sacrificially.[300] Because Jesus knew, as E. Stanley Jones observes, that "abundant living depends upon abundant giving."[301]

So give. Give money. Give time. Give stuff. Give freely. Give generously. Give extravagantly. As Leonard Sweet writes:

> When I write a check or set up an automatic withdrawal or toss some cash into the offering plate, I am not disbursing my assets but God's. I am making a theological decision about how much to receive for myself of what is God's based on Jesus' admonition "Freely ye have received, freely give" (Matthew 10:8 KJV). How do we make this decision?
>
> One thing to remember is that our God is an extravagant God (Ephesians 3:20; Philippians 4:19). God has lavished on us an incredible trust. Will you become God's trustee? Will you receive the estate God has in store for you?
>
> I'm not ascetic. I don't romanticize poverty. I enjoy life. I champion an elegant spirituality.
>
> "Elegant" is now a technical term among physicists used to advocate certain theories. To clinch a case, they say, "It's an elegant formulation." By this they mean that it is internally consistent, analytically comprehensive, coherently polished, beautiful of design and expression, respectful of mystery, and capable of engendering wonder and awe.
>
> Jesus champions for us an "elegant" life. [302]

An elegant life is a giving life. A generous life. A magnanimous life. A blessed, extravagant life that comes to its fullest bloom. . .in giving.

GIVE PRESENCE

The innkeeper (or his wife or daughter, perhaps) gave hospitality that first Christmas. Mary and Joseph gave the gift of availability. The magi gave gold, frankincense, and myrrh. But what did Jesus give? He was just a babe in a manger. He didn't exactly have the opportunity to dash down to Wal-Mart on Christmas Eve. He was otherwise occupied, you might say.

But still, Jesus gave the best gift of all: himself. . .his presence. He managed to squeeze his eternity into human infancy; and though he owned the world and everything in it, he showed up as a newborn babe. He gave not "presents," but "presence."

He came. He showed up. He walked beside. He sat with. He listened. He attended. He noticed.

Often the best gift we can give is the gift of presence. When Job suffered crushing losses and afflictions—not just the loss of property and possessions, but of his health and his children—the Bible says that his friends came and sat with him:

> *When Job's three friends, Eliphaz the Temanite, Bildad the Shuhite, and Zophar the Naamathite, heard about all the troubles that had come upon him, they set out from their homes and met together by agreement to go and sympathize with him and comfort him. When they saw him from a distance, they could hardly recognize him; they began to weep aloud, and they tore their robes and sprinkled dust on their heads. Then they sat on the ground with him for seven days and seven nights. No one said a word to him, because they saw how great his suffering was.* [303]

Seven days and seven nights of silence. Tears. Presence. They later spoiled it by opening their mouths, but their presence is still a gift we would do well to emulate. So give presence. Sit with someone who is hurting. Sit beside someone in church. Put aside the laptop and color with your kids. Show up at weddings and funerals. Visit a patient in a hospital or nursing home (even if you can't be sure they know you are there). Be there for someone. Listen. Attend. Notice.

Give as the innkeeper gave. As Mary and Joseph gave. As the magi did. As Jesus did. . .and does.

THE FINAL WORD

The phone rang late one night. Jim, his wife, and his children had already gone to bed. He rolled over, stretched an arm out of the tangle of sheets, snatched the phone receiver out of the cradle, and said hello. Though he was groggy, Jim recognized the voice on the other end of the line as that of an old friend.

The friend was calling from several time zones away. "I'm sorry for calling so late, old buddy, but I just had to give you something."

"Give me something?" Jim was awake now.

"Yes! I don't know if I ever told you about this or not, but back when I was in college, I promised myself—and God, I guess—that I would give something away every single day of my life."

"You're kidding."

"It's not always a big deal. Sometimes I give a quarter to a kid who lost his money in a candy machine, or I give a book I've enjoyed to someone I think will like it. But every day now, for the past fifteen years, I don't think I've missed a single day."

"You've given something away every day for the last fifteen years?"

"Yup! And I realized just a few minutes ago that I hadn't given anything away yet today, so I thought I'd call you."

"What are you going to give me over the phone?"

"Well, old buddy, I can't give you a kiss, now, can I? But I can give you this—it may not be much, but it's something." He read a short poem over the phone, explaining the godly influence his distant friend had had on him. When he stopped reading, silence hung between the two men.

"Thanks," Jim said finally. His voice quivered with emotion. "That's the best gift I've gotten in a long time."

Imagine giving something away every day for fifteen years! It may seem incredible, but it is not impossible, as that true account suggests. The final word for this chapter is to *give something* every day this week. Or, if you are feeling ambitious, extend it to a month. Or more. It's up to you. But whatever you give each day—and for how long—do your best to heed these words from Jesus: "Give as freely as you have received!"[304]

THE WORD OF INCLUSION

No one likes to be left out.

Maybe you knew the childhood heartbreak of standing, waiting, hoping while sides were chosen for baseball or basketball or kickball. Maybe you remember the sinking feeling as one kid after another was chosen, leaving you among the last to be picked. Maybe you even experienced the humiliation of one of the team captains surrendering the last pick by telling the other team captain, "You can have him (or her)."

Maybe you've shown up for one job interview after another, only to hear the disappointing news, "We've hired someone else," or "We've decided to go a different direction." Perhaps you have seen people whispering in your presence as a way of keeping you out of the loop or out of the group. You may even have experienced the sting of racism, sexism, or other forms of bigotry and exclusion.

Exclusion is a horrible thing. It always hurts. And it often leaves scars. Social psychologist Kipling D. Williams writes in *Scientific American*:

> *Studies reveal that even subtle, artificial, or ostensibly unimportant exclusion can lead to strong emotional reactions. A strong reaction makes sense when your spouse's family or close circle of friends rejects or shuns you, because these people are important to you. It is more surprising that important instances of being barred are not necessary for intense feelings of rejection to emerge. We can feel awful even after people we have never met simply look the other way.*
>
> *This reaction serves a function: it warns us that something*

is wrong, that there exists a serious threat to our social and psychological well-being. Psychologists Roy Baumeister of Florida State University and Mark Leary of Duke University had argued in a 1995 article that belonging to a group was a need—not a desire or preference—and, when thwarted, leads to psychological and physical illness.. . .

Ostracism uniquely threatens all these needs. Even in a verbal or physical altercation, individuals are still connected. Total exclusion, however, severs all bonds. Social rejection also deals a uniquely harsh blow to self-esteem, because it implies wrongdoing. Worse, the imposed silence forces us to ruminate, generating self-deprecating thoughts in our search for an explanation. The forced isolation also makes us feel helpless: you can fight back, but no one will respond. Finally, ostracism makes our very existence feel less meaningful because this type of rejection makes us feel invisible and unimportant. [305]

Jesus' word of inclusion is as necessary and welcome today as it was two thousand years ago—perhaps even more so. It is a word for everyone who has responded to Jesus' first word—"Come"—and a word that turns his followers outward into a world that is filled with hurting, alienated, and ostracized people. The word: *bring.*

A BRINGER OF MEN

Rooms full of books have been written over the years about Jesus' first followers—the Twelve, as the Gospels sometimes call them. Many point out the clear symbolism in his choice of twelve men—not eleven, not thirteen, but twelve—by which he signaled the ushering in of the kingdom of God and the creation of a New Israel (the people of Israel had constituted twelve tribes out of the sons of Jacob, or Israel).

An added wrinkle of that conglomeration of twelve men

Jesus called to follow him is that it made room for many different personalities and temperaments. Perhaps not everyone can identify with Peter, the impulsive fisherman who always seemed to be at the front, answering questions, speaking out of turn, and even wielding an untimely sword. Nor would everyone feel a kinship with John, perhaps the youngest of the band, who may have been Jesus' closest friend on earth. Or Matthew, also called Levi, who had a head for numbers, or Simon the Zealot, who had been an active anti-Roman insurgent. And so on.

Similarly, not everyone would identify with Andrew, Peter's brother, who (perhaps more than anyone) seemed early on to fulfill Jesus' plan for his followers to be "fishers of men."[306] In fact, though Andrew seems to play a bit part in the Gospels of Matthew, Mark, and Luke (the first three Gospels to be written and distributed), the Gospel of John seems to make it a point to shine a light on Andrew's penchant for bringing people to Jesus.

Here's how the first chapter of John introduces Andrew:

> *The next day John was there again with two of his disciples.*
> *When he saw Jesus passing by, he said, "Look, the Lamb of God!"*
> *When the two disciples heard him say this, they followed Jesus. Turning around, Jesus saw them following and asked, "What do you want?"*
> *They said, "Rabbi" (which means "Teacher"), "where are you staying?"*
> *"Come," he replied, "and you will see."*
> *So they went and saw where he was staying, and they spent that day with him. It was about four in the afternoon.*
> *Andrew, Simon Peter's brother, was one of the two who heard what John had said and who had followed Jesus. The first thing Andrew did was to find his brother Simon and tell him, "We have found the Messiah" (that is, the Christ). And he*

brought him to Jesus. [307]

The *first thing* Andrew did, upon following Jesus himself, was to find his brother, Simon Peter, and bring him to Jesus. And that was only the beginning.

On another occasion, a crowd of thousands had gathered on a Galilean slope to hear Jesus teach, and as the day wore on, Jesus suggested that his closest followers find a way to feed them. John's Gospel reports:

> *Philip answered him, "It would take more than half a year's wages to buy enough bread for each one to have a bite!"*
>
> *Another of his disciples, Andrew, Simon Peter's brother, spoke up, "Here is a boy with five small barley loaves and two small fish, but how far will they go among so many?"* [308]

The Bible never tells us how Andrew knew about the boy and his lunch, but that is not the point. The point is that Andrew brought the boy to Jesus, and in so doing he paved the way for a miracle.

On still another occasion, after Jesus had entered the holy city of Jerusalem, riding on a donkey, to the shouts and cheers of the crowds that had assembled for the upcoming Passover festival, Andrew was at the center of an effort to bring people to Jesus:

> *Now there were some Greeks among those who went up to worship at the festival. They came to Philip, who was from Bethsaida in Galilee, with a request. "Sir," they said, "we would like to see Jesus." Philip went to tell Andrew; Andrew and Philip in turn told Jesus.* [309]

Interesting, isn't it, that Philip—one of the Twelve—went to

Andrew with the visitors' request? He presumably had just as much access to Jesus as Andrew did, and he had personally brought at least one other person to Jesus. [310] But whatever his reasons, he referred the request to Andrew, who then accompanied Philip to tell Jesus about the people who wanted to meet him.

Perhaps John, in his Gospel, intends for us to see how it is done. How an ordinary guy like Andrew can be remembered for bringing people to Jesus. How any one of us can fulfill Jesus' mandate. Timeless, effective ways that each of us can hear and obey the word of inclusion: *bring*.

EXTEND ACCEPTANCE

In Jesus' day, a rabbi couldn't be too careful for his reputation. He would accept only the most qualified students. He would cultivate and guard his standing in the community. He would assiduously avoid contact with women, corpses, and dogs. He would never be so undignified as to run or hurry. And children—children could pose a special problem. Sometimes fussy, often loud, and always unpredictable, children could interrupt a rabbi's teaching and threaten his dignity like few other things.

But not if the rabbi was Jesus:

> *One day children were brought to Jesus in the hope that he would lay hands on them and pray over them. The disciples shooed them off. But Jesus intervened: "Let the children alone, don't prevent them from coming to me. God's kingdom is made up of people like these." After laying hands on them, he left.* [311]

In Mark's account of the same incident, he uses a word used nowhere else to describe Jesus. Mark says that Jesus was "displeased" or "indignant" when his disciples tried to keep the little children away from him. Jesus made a point of accepting and affirming the most vulnerable and unpredictable kind of people imaginable: children. He had to know they would squirm and squeal and spit up, but he accepted them nonetheless. Or all the more.

Jesus' example suggests that we ought to do the same in bringing others into our circles of influence, into places where they might meet Jesus and experience his loving touch. Sure, they might be messy. They might be rough around the edges. They might disrupt things. But Jesus says to bring them anyway. Extend acceptance to them. Don't insist that they have to grow up or clean up or dress up before they can be included. Include them nonetheless—or all the more.

EXPRESS INTEREST

One day, Jesus was traveling through Samaria with his closest followers. He came to a well outside a town called Sychar.

> When a Samaritan woman came to draw water, Jesus said to her, "Will you give me a drink?" (His disciples had gone into the town to buy food.)
>
> The Samaritan woman said to him, "You are a Jew and I am a Samaritan woman. How can you ask me for a drink?" (For Jews do not associate with Samaritans.) [312]

Obviously, the woman was surprised that Jesus spoke to her, because (a) Jewish men did not talk to women in public, (b) Jews did not associate with Samaritans, and (c) Jews did not share cups or pitchers with non-Jews.

But Jesus did.

Not only did he talk to her, but he used his own thirst to initiate a spiritual conversation with someone in need. He said, "Will you give me a drink?"

Now, remember: This is a guy who could walk on water. He

could command storms. He could have summoned a tidy little rain cloud to come and perch over his head so that all he had to do was lift his face to the sky, open his mouth, and let the cloud squirt a few convenient gulps of water down his throat. He even could have beckoned a sweet, pretty hummingbird to fly past afterward and dry his lips with a few beats of its tiny wings.

But he didn't.

He said, "Will you give me a drink?"

He could have slaked his thirst in a million different ways, but he chose to say to a Samaritan woman, of all people, "Will you give me a drink?"

Because his request not only initiated a meaningful conversation—it placed him in a position to ask and receive something from her.

That's wisdom.

Most people today see "church folk" as people who "have all the answers"—or at least *think* they do. People who want to sell something, even if it's free. If you've ever participated in "servant evangelism,"[313] such as giving away free soda or water in a public park, or going door-to-door to hand out fresh batteries for smoke alarms, you know that there are always some people who will say no, even when they know they're being offered something free. They may think there's a catch, or they may just be reluctant to receive something from a stranger—and there's no one stranger, they may think, than "church folk." For those very reasons, however, such efforts can often start spiritual conversations and invite people to look at "church folk" in a new way.

Jesus went beyond that. He started his dialogue with the Samaritan woman from a whole different perspective. He approached her as someone with something to offer *him*, before revealing that he had something to offer her.

That's a helpful example for those of us who would heed Jesus' word to *bring* others closer to him. If the Son of God could place himself in a position to receive something—anything—from someone who was far from God, maybe we can express a healthy interest in what our neighbors and colleagues and acquaintances have to offer. Maybe it would open some surprising dialogues and initiate some real give-and-take relationships with the people around us, the people who are already in our sphere of influence, the people we know. . .but not really.

It might mean asking your coworker someday, "How do you stay so trim and fit? What can I learn from you?" Or maybe you ask another mom in your MOPS group, "Are you always as calm as you seem? What's your secret?" Or maybe, just maybe, to the person down the row from you at church, "You know, I've seen you here for a long time, but I don't think I've ever asked your name. Tell me about yourself."

Sure, you may be way too shy for that, and that's okay. But there is surely some way for you to express an interest in—and even initiate some real give-and-take with—someone. Not being nosy. Not getting into their business. Just expressing an interest and maybe sincerely asking them for some help or advice. If Jesus could do it, why not you?

SHOW RESPECT

Jesus also taught a way of bringing people closer to the kingdom of God by showing respect. It is a theme interwoven with another of his favorite topics—humility. It takes a humble heart to demonstrate respect for others, which is crucial to fulfilling Jesus' desire for us to be "bringers of men and women."

Once, when Jesus was invited to the house of a "prominent Pharisee," he took the opportunity to drive this point home to his followers:

When [Jesus] noticed how the guests picked the places of honor

at the table, he told them this parable: "When someone invites
you to a wedding feast, do not take the place of honor, for a
person more distinguished than you may have been invited. If
so, the host who invited both of you will come and say to you,
'Give this person your seat.' Then, humiliated, you will have
to take the least important place. But when you are invited,
take the lowest place, so that when your host comes, he will
say to you, 'Friend, move up to a better place.' Then you will
be honored in the presence of all the other guests. For all those
who exalt themselves will be humbled, and those who humble
themselves will be exalted." [314]

Jesus clearly appeals to self-interest with his words: "It's better
to humble yourself and then be exalted, than to exalt yourself,
only to be humbled." But something else is also in play here. Jesus
says to keep in mind that "a person more distinguished than you
may have been invited."

This attitude of humility is clearly in keeping with the life
and mission of Jesus himself, who said, "The Son of Man. . .came
to serve, not to be served—and then to give away his life."[315]
He treated women with respect—even a Samaritan woman. He
treated foreigners with respect—even a woman from Tyre. He
treated a Roman centurion with respect. Tax collectors. Beggars.
Prostitutes.

And he enjoins his followers to do the same. It will bring hearts
closer to him. It will open doors to the Gospel. It will pave the way
to the kingdom for someone.

ADD VALUE

Matthew's account of the feeding of the five thousand doesn't
mention Andrew's agency in bringing the boy with the loaves and
fishes to Jesus. But it does add one helpful detail. After the disciples

"informed" Jesus (as if he really had to be told) that they had "only five loaves here and two fish,"[316] he said, "Bring them here to me."[317]

On another occasion, a man dropped to his knees before Jesus, asking him to heal his son, who suffered from frequent and violent seizures. He had brought the boy to the Twelve, but they had tried and failed to help the boy. After expressing frustration with his faithless disciples, Jesus said, "Bring him here to me"[318]—and then healed the boy.

On each occasion, Jesus issued the word of inclusion—*bring*—in order to perform a miracle, an act that met people's needs. In that tiny detail, there is a message for us.

Somewhere along the line, many of us who follow Christ have gotten things backward or inside out. Most of our "bringing" in recent generations has been to gatherings that most of the general public don't feel a need for—revivals and tent meetings and the like—or to fund-raising and fleecing events (church festivals, bake sales, fund-raising dinners, concerts, etc.).

Some churches have begun to reverse this pattern by purposefully and pointedly refusing to sell anything, either at their church or at events sponsored by the church. That is a great start.

But notice that Jesus went well beyond that. He gave stuff away. He added value to people everywhere he went. And not just "religious" things. Practical things. Like lunch for thousands on a hillside. Tax payments from the mouth of a fish. Healings and resurrections.

So when Jesus says, "Bring," he's not asking his followers to get sponsors for seats at a fund-raiser. He's not hawking tickets to a Christian movie or concert. He wants us to give valuable things to people—not just things they *should* value, but things they already *do* value. When his followers do that, it awakens people's interest in the other things his followers are doing. Things such as food and healing incite interest in things such as forgiveness and salvation, love and community. When we bring people to things that meet their felt needs, we help move them toward feeling and expressing deeper needs, often before they even understand or recognize their deeper need.

HAVE FUN

One of the most meaningful and effective ways to bring people closer to the kingdom of God is to celebrate with them. Jesus repeatedly encouraged his followers to bring people of all kinds to celebrations of all kinds:

> *Jesus said to his host, "When you give a luncheon or dinner, do not invite your friends, your brothers or sisters, your relatives, or your rich neighbors; if you do, they may invite you back and so you will be repaid. But when you give a banquet, invite the poor, the crippled, the lame, the blind, and you will be blessed. Although they cannot repay you, you will be repaid at the resurrection of the righteous."[319]*

It is no accident that Jesus' contemporaries saw him as a party animal. He never sinned, but he apparently accepted more party invitations than most rabbis of his time. From all accounts, he loved a good party. For instance:

> *While Jesus was having dinner at Matthew's house, many tax collectors and sinners came and ate with him and his disciples. When the Pharisees saw this, they asked his disciples, "Why does your teacher eat with tax collectors and sinners?"[320]*

Jesus had such a fondness for partying with people of all types—even the "wrong" crowd—that it got people's tongues wagging. He even acknowledged the gossip about him, saying, "The Son of Man came eating and drinking, and they say, 'Here is a glutton and a drunkard, a friend of tax collectors and sinners.' But wisdom is proved right by her deeds."[321]

He didn't just "fellowship" with the religious crowd. He included everyone—"the poor, the crippled, the lame, the blind," and even the rough-around-the-edges—and they clearly enjoyed being around him.

So if you would heed Jesus' word of inclusion, have some fun. Invite people of all stripes—and spots—into your fun. Join in their fun. It doesn't even have to be a church-sponsored event! As Jesus' example shows us, having fun with people can be a wise and fruitful way of *bringing* them closer to the kingdom of God.

THE FINAL WORD
Richard Rohr writes:

> *Those at the edge of any system and those excluded from any system ironically and invariably hold the secret for the conversion and wholeness of that very group. They always hold the feared, rejected, and denied parts of the group's soul. You see, therefore, why the church was meant to be that group that constantly went to the edges, to the "least of the brothers and sisters," and even to the enemy. Jesus was not just a theological genius, but he was also a psychological and sociological genius. When any church defines itself by exclusion of anybody, it is always wrong. It is avoiding its only vocation, which is to be the Christ. The only groups that Jesus seriously critiques are those who include themselves and exclude others from the always-given grace of God.*
>
> *Only as the People of God receive the stranger, the sinner, and the immigrant, those who don't play our game our way, do we discover not only the hidden, feared, and hated parts of*

*our own souls, but the fullness of Jesus himself. We need them
for our own conversion.* [322]

The last word in this chapter is simple: Bring someone on the outside inside. Include someone who is usually excluded. Do it in a small way (such as inviting someone into a conversation) or a big way (such as throwing a party in honor of someone who is usually excluded). But do it (or schedule it) before the sun goes down today.

15

THE WORD THAT STOOPS

"I just feel so useless."

The man who spoke those words to me had just suffered a setback. He had applied for one job after another, and though he had repeatedly been a finalist candidate, he had been turned down again. It was disheartening.

I should have been more sensitive. I had encouraged and supported him throughout his struggles to find "meaningful" employment. I'm not even sure why I said what I did in that moment, except that his words seemed to ignite something inside me.

"There's no excuse for that," I said.

He blinked at me like I had just smacked him. But I didn't apologize or back down. "Sure, you're not getting the jobs you want. You've been trying really hard, sending out résumés, going on interviews. And so far it has produced nothing. That's disappointing. I'm disappointed *for* you and *with* you. But there's no excuse for feeling useless. None. Just because no one has hired you doesn't mean you shouldn't be working. There are all sorts of places where you can serve, all sorts of people who need help you can give, in one way or another. Maybe not in a job that 'floats your boat,' and maybe not even for money. But if you're feeling useless, it's not the fault of the job market, and it's not the fault of potential employers or hiring committees. It's your fault."

What I didn't add, but could have, was this: "Because dirty feet are everywhere."

A ROOM WITH A P.U.

They arrived in groups of twos and threes, talking loudly, laughing boisterously.

They were Galileans, all but one, and they were men of the sea, men of the soil, and a couple were men of the sword.

They were all disciples of the teacher and miracle-worker called Jesus, or Yeshua; and they entered, several at a time, into the upper room of the house in Jerusalem where they'd met before.

Jesus entered in the midst of them, and in the space of just a few minutes, all had assembled in the rectangular room with the low ceiling.

Suddenly, however, something changed. Faces that, moments earlier, had been animated—smiling, laughing, talking—now reflected uncertainty and discomfort. Though no one spoke, everyone in the room faced the same predicament. Everyone felt the same awkward apprehension.

You see, the roads and alleys that these men had traveled on their way to this "upper room" were not paved roads. In fact, in many cities and towns of that time and place, paved roads were unheard of. The streets these men trod were more like winding dirt trails, all covered with a thick layer of dust. Therefore, it was the custom for the host of a home to station a servant at the door to wash the feet of the dinner guests as they arrived. The servant knelt with a pitcher of water, a pan, and a towel, and washed the dirt or mud off the feet of each guest as he or she prepared to enter the home. Shoes and sandals were left at the door.

If a home could not afford a servant, it was customary for one of the early arriving guests to take upon himself the role of the servant and wash the feet of those who arrived after him. To enter a place such as the upper room or approach a meal with unwashed feet was to them like entering a restaurant barefoot might feel to us.

So, though no one spoke of it, everyone had the same thought: Someone really should wash their feet.

In the midst of the stilted conversation that revealed their discomfort, Jesus—their teacher, their rabbi—strode quietly to the low table that occupied the center of the room.

The table was surrounded by cushioned couches, the head of each couch placed against the table like thirteen spokes in a wheel. Jesus took his place at the table, reclining on one elbow, in such a position where he could survey all twelve of the men he had chosen to follow him.

And all twelve slowly, as casually as they could manage, chose their places on the couches around the table. . .leaving the servant's pitcher, pan, and towel undisturbed by the door.

The table was spread with plates and cups, and the fragrance of the roast lamb, herbs, and bread mingled with the odor of the unwashed feet that hung over the ends of the couches.

A few awkward moments passed. After the last man had taken his place on the one remaining couch, Jesus, without saying a word, slipped away from the table, silently pulled off his outer tunic, and tied the long servant's towel around his waist. Then, with pitcher and pan in hand, he knelt at the feet of the disciple nearest him.

What little hushed conversation there had been now ceased altogether.

Jesus moved quietly from man to man while every eye in the room followed him.

The disciples were speechless while he quickly and efficiently performed the servant's task, first pouring water from the pitcher over each pair of feet, allowing the basin on the floor beneath to catch the water and dirt that flowed down, then wiping the man's feet dry with the towel he had wrapped around his waist as an apron.

Having tenderly wiped the feet of Andrew, Jesus moved to the next couch, the one occupied by Peter.

Peter, visibly disturbed, drew his feet up onto the couch. "Lord, are *you* going to wash *my* feet?"

Reaching out a hand, Jesus gripped one of Peter's feet and

pulled it back to the edge of the couch. "You do not realize now what I am doing. But later you will understand."

Peter once again drew his feet away from Jesus. His voice when he spoke was half pleading, half insisting. "No! You shall never wash my feet."

Jesus saw Peter's pride disguised as humility. He looked up and peered into the fisherman's eyes. "Unless I wash you, you have no part with me."

Jesus' words were quiet but left no room for argument. Peter locked gazes with Jesus for a long moment. "Then, Lord," he said finally, "not just my feet but my hands and my head as well!"

Jesus reached out tenderly, took Peter's heel in his hand, and resumed his task of washing. Matter-of-factly, without looking up from his chore, he referred to the custom of those days of bathing before going to a banquet so that, upon arrival, only the guests' feet, dusty from the journey, needed to be washed. "A person who has had a bath needs only to wash his feet; his whole body is clean. And you are clean—" He looked around the room. "Though not every one of you."

A few minutes later, he had washed the feet of all twelve sheepish, embarrassed disciples. He returned the pitcher, towel, and basin to their place by the door. Then, while every pair of eyes in the room watched, he walked back to his place at the table. He stood beside the low sofa and looked around the company of the Twelve.

"Do you understand what I have done for you?"

No one answered. It seemed obvious.

"You call me 'Teacher' and 'Lord,' and rightly so, for that is what I am. Now that I, your Lord and Teacher, have washed your feet, you also should wash one another's feet. I have set you an example that you should do as I have done for you."[323]

As each man in the room heard those words, he no doubt recalled those moments when he had first arrived, when he was too proud to take the basin and towel in hand and serve the others.

NONSELECTIVE SERVICE

That scene describes what happened just before Jesus predicted his betrayal at his last supper. It presented one last opportunity for Jesus to drive home a point he had made frequently to his followers.

> *"You know that the rulers of the Gentiles lord it over them, and their high officials exercise authority over them. Not so with you. Instead, whoever wants to become great among you must be your servant, and whoever wants to be first must be your slave—just as the Son of Man did not come to be served, but to serve, and to give his life as a ransom for many."* [324]

On another occasion, Jesus told his followers, "Anyone who wants to be first must be the very last, and the servant of all," [325] and "The greatest among you will be your servant." [326]

So when, just hours before his arrest and trial, Jesus tells them, "Now that I, your Lord and Teacher, have washed your feet, you also should wash one another's feet," it couldn't have been a surprise to them. It wasn't new information. He had repeatedly spoken to them the word that stoops: *serve.*

It is a word he speaks to us, too. He says it to all of his followers. He says it to you.

Serve.

If our Lord and teacher washed the feet of his *talmidim*, we can wash the feet of others, too. If the Son of Man did not come to be served, but to serve, we can serve too. If the Incarnate Word was not too dignified to stoop, to kneel, to get his hands dirty, how can we claim that any task is beneath us? There should be no task, no role, and no effort that we will not do for others.

Samuel Logan Brengle was an accomplished orator who had been offered a highly prestigious position in a large Methodist church. So when he traveled to England to offer his services to

William Booth, the founder of the Salvation Army, Brengle was surprised that Booth expressed reservations. "You belong to the 'dangerous classes,' " Booth said. "You've been your own boss so long that I don't think you'll want to submit to Salvation Army discipline."[327] Worse, on his second day at the Salvation Army's training college, Brengle was assigned to polish the boots of the other cadets in training:

> *The devil came at me, and reminded me that I had graduated from a university, had attended a leading theological school, had been pastor of a metropolitan church, had just left evangelistic work in which I saw hundreds seeking the Savior, and that now I was only blacking boots for a lot of ignorant lads. But I reminded my old enemy of the example of my Lord, and he left me, and that little cellar was changed into one of heaven's anterooms, and my Lord visited me there.* [328]

It is a word easily forgotten. And it is not enough to say, "Oh, sure, I would scrub floors for my brother," or "I wouldn't hesitate to serve others." Jesus didn't say, "I have set you an example that you should be *willing* to do as I have done for you." He didn't say, "I have set you an example that you should *agree in theory* with what I have done for you." He said, "I have set you an example that you should *do* as I have done for you."[329]

Whether you are willing or not, if you are not serving others, you are not following Christ. Whether you agree or not, if you are not stooping to serve, you are not obeying his word. Jesus says to you, "Serve."

SURPRISE OTHERS BY SERVING THEM

Serving others can be some of the most fun you'll ever have—particularly as people are taken off-balance by your kindness and thoughtfulness.

Chuck had only a nodding acquaintance with his next-door neighbors, but he knew that Keith had recently been laid off and had taken a job that required a lot of travel. So one day when Chuck finished mowing his lawn, he kept right on going into Keith's yard. A week or two later, he saw Keith's wife, Melissa, in the grocery store and she told him—in tears—how much that simple act of service had helped her and her husband.

Derrick, a college student, always clears his friends' cups and dishes from the cafeteria table as he clears his own. When Andrea sees an older couple eating in a restaurant, she likes to secretly pay for their meal; sometimes she will even stick around to watch the expression on their faces when they're informed that someone paid for their meal. Jim does something similar; a frequent customer at Starbucks, he delights in asking the person behind him in line what he or she plans to order and then paying for it when he buys his own coffee.

Surprising others by serving them doesn't have to take extra time or cost money, either. It can be as easy as giving an unexpected compliment or returning a shopping cart for someone. It can be as simple as giving your newspaper to the person at the next table when you get up to leave the coffee shop. On the other hand, it can be as extravagant as spending a day helping someone move, or driving several hours to sit with someone during their chemo treatments.

Be careful, though, because surprising others by serving them can become addictive. It fosters joy and blessing in your life, even as you shower it on others. Even the lowest, grimiest tasks—like washing someone's feet or weeding someone's garden—can turn a cellar into heaven's anteroom or a patch of dirt into holy ground.

SERVE OTHERS IN TRANSFORMING WAYS

It is human nature to seek to serve others in ways that enhance our own self-image and preserve our own sensibilities. Samuel Logan Brengle sincerely sought to serve others by preaching God's Word in prestigious pulpits, but polishing shoes was a transformative experience in his life. It was out of the norm for him. It seemed like an insult at first. It challenged him. And, possibly because of those very things, it changed him.

What sorts of service to others seem insulting to you? What would most likely prompt you to say, "I would never do that"? Those sorts of experiences are likely to be the most transformative and rewarding kinds of service you can offer. They force you to rely on God's power rather than your own resources. They introduce you to new ways of thinking and acting. They have the potential to change the way you see yourself—and others around you.

René is a millionaire. His corner office, penthouse suite, and many employees keep his daily life comfortable and secure. His schedule is filled with concerts, banquets, and balls. But he hadn't always been wealthy. One day, when he realized that his life had become insulated, he called a Manhattan soup kitchen and volunteered to help. When he arrived, he was handed an apron, plastic gloves, and a large serving spoon and was directed to the food line, where he dished out green beans for nearly an hour. He came back the next day and soon was a regular in the serving line. He got to know the street people and the working poor in that area of town. And it changed him. It made him "feel more human," he said. And though he was not a particularly religious man when he started, he felt faith begin to stir somewhere inside of him.

Something similar must have happened to Jesus' first followers after their humbling experience in the upper room. Years later, Peter—who at first had tried to refuse Jesus' servant ministry to him—seemed to remember the incident with great clarity. In writing a letter to the church scattered across Asia Minor, he told them, in a pointed reference to Jesus' act of wrapping the servant's towel around himself before washing his disciples' feet, "All of you must put on the apron of humility, to serve one another; for the scripture says, 'God resists the proud, but shows favor to the humble.'" [330]

As you serve others, take on tasks that stretch you and challenge you. Consider the kinds of service that may test you, because those may be some of the most transforming experiences of your life.

SERVE JESUS AS YOU SERVE OTHERS

There is a detail in John 13 that is easily overlooked and often missed altogether. See if you can find it. Go ahead, take a few moments and open your Bible. Turn to John 13 and look at verses 1-20. See if you can find the answer to this question:

Who washed Jesus' feet?

Did you find it? Do you see the answer? Verse 12 says, "When he had finished washing their feet, he put on his clothes and returned to his place." [331]

Twelve men got their feet washed that day. But there were thirteen men in the room.

From all appearances, Jesus returned to his place at the table with unwashed feet. The answer to the question is evidently, "No one." No one washed Jesus' feet. Even after his unforgettable demonstration, none of the Twelve got up from his seat to wash Jesus' feet.

To be fair, they were all probably a little shell-shocked. Humiliated. Who wouldn't be? The Son of God, the Creator of all things, had just washed their feet. . .because they were too proud to serve each other. But still. . .

Do you remember when Jesus spoke of feeding the hungry and clothing the poor and visiting those who are sick and in prison? Do you remember that he said, "Whatever you did for one of the least of these brothers and sisters of mine, you did for me,"[332] and "Whatever you did not do for one of the least of these, you did not do for me"?[333]

What if Jesus went back to that table with dirty feet because—in some mysterious but real way—when his followers do not serve each other, Jesus himself pays the price of their pride? What if, when you and I do not serve each other—because we're unwilling to forgive, because we won't swallow our pride, because the task is somehow beneath us, because it's easier to let someone else do it, whatever the reason—Jesus feels it?

Notice that he did not say, "Whatever you did for one of the least of these brothers and sisters of mine, *it is as if* you did it for me." That is how we tend to read it or hear it, but that is not what he said. He said, "Whatever you did for one of the least of these brothers and sisters of mine, *you did for me*." Or didn't do.

So when you wash the feet of another, when you humbly serve a brother or sister, when you give and expect nothing in return, when you cook a meal, shovel a sidewalk, offer a ride, mop a floor, empty a bedpan, surrender the spotlight, deflect the credit, shoulder the blame, share the burden, you are blessing not only that person; you are blessing the very heart of Jesus. According to his words, you are not just doing it on his behalf; you are doing it *to him*.

What if you took that to heart? What if you served in that awareness? What if you woke up tomorrow and believed that your service to other people was truly and literally service to Jesus himself?

THE FINAL WORD

Jesus says, not only to the Twelve, but to you and me, "Do as I have done. Wash one another's feet. Serve others in love."

The final word in this chapter is easy.

Stoop.

Do *one thing* today that serves another person. One thing that requires you to humble yourself. To go out of your way. To bow a little lower than you're accustomed to. Maybe even a lot lower.

You may plan it, or you may wing it.

But if the sun sets another day before you can honestly say you have been a servant to someone, don't go on to the next chapter until you've heeded the word that stoops.

THE WORD THAT CLINGS

It is called "attachment disorder."

It occurs when a child has been hindered from regularly connecting with a parent or primary caregiver. For example, if a newborn cries for long periods of time and no one responds or offers comfort; if a baby is isolated from positive human contact for long stretches—receiving no caresses, talking, singing, or smiling; if a young child is neglected or abused and receives attention only by misbehaving, and so on, it can make it difficult for that child, over the course of his or her life, to connect emotionally with other people. He or she will seem aloof and insensitive to others and will tend to feel unsafe and alone, insecure and powerless.

Something like that happens sometimes in the spiritual realm as well.

Just as a baby is born physically, so a person may also experience a spiritual birth, something Jesus called being "born again." It is a wonderful thing. A life-changing moment. A fresh start.

But if that new life is not nurtured and cared for in important, constructive ways, a sort of "spiritual attachment disorder" can occur. Jesus said:

> *"I am the true vine, and my Father is the vinedresser. Every branch in me that does not bear fruit he takes away, and every branch that does bear fruit he prunes, that it may bear more fruit. Already you are clean because of the word that I have spoken to you. Abide in me, and I in you. As the branch cannot bear fruit by itself, unless it abides in the vine, neither can you, unless you abide in me. I am the vine; you are the*

branches. Whoever abides in me and I in him, he it is that bears much fruit, for apart from me you can do nothing. If anyone does not abide in me he is thrown away like a branch and withers; and the branches are gathered, thrown into the fire, and burned. If you abide in me, and my words abide in you, ask whatever you wish, and it will be done for you. By this my Father is glorified, that you bear much fruit and so prove to be my disciples. As the Father has loved me, so have I loved you. Abide in my love. If you keep my commandments, you will abide in my love, just as I have kept my Father's commandments and abide in his love. These things I have spoken to you, that my joy may be in you, and that your joy may be full." [334]

Long before "attachment disorder" was classified and cataloged, Jesus made it clear to his first followers that attachment—like the shoot of a grapevine connecting to the trunk—is absolutely necessary to the soul that has experienced new life through Jesus Christ. He said, "Apart from me you can do nothing." [335] In other words, your soul's attachment to Jesus is the key—to joy, to love, and to all of the fruit that is produced by the healthy Christian life.

SPIRITUAL ATTACHMENT DISORDER

Unfortunately, however, attachment is not automatic. Just as an infant needs early, frequent, and positive contact with a parent or caregiver, so the "newborn" Christian needs early, frequent, and positive contact with Jesus in order to form the attachment that will produce lasting joy, abiding love, and ongoing fruit in the Christian life. Often this kind of contact is provided by a caring mentor, a loving teacher or pastor, or a healthy small group or church community. Those kinds of contact can be used by the Holy Spirit to foster a new Christian's prayer life, worship experience, and study habits in ways that will promote growth and bear fruit for a lifetime.

But that is not always the case. Sometimes a new Christian cries out for help and no one responds. Occasionally a "babe in Christ" is isolated from positive contact with other Christians for long stretches. Other times, a young follower of Jesus is abused in some way. And sometimes initial efforts of mentors, pastors, and churches are somehow derailed, and detachment occurs along the way.

But whether or not you have ever experienced the "abiding in the Vine" kind of intimacy Jesus speaks of in John 15, you can still heed his words. You can begin—or begin again—to "abide" in him. You can fully, freely, and consistently experience the joy, love, and fruit that flows from the abiding life.

ATTACH

To state the obvious: Before we can *abide* in Christ, we must first *attach* to him. This happens, of course, when the sinful heart and soul cries out, "Be merciful to me, a sinner!"[336] Sin is confessed, repented of, and forgiven. The life is surrendered to Jesus, who enters in and imparts a new heart and a new spirit.[337] The old passes away; everything is made new.[338]

F. B. Meyer writes:

One day when traveling by train, a young man sat opposite me in the car, reading Thomas à Kempis' Imitation of Christ. I knew the book, and sat beside him and said, "A grand book."
He said, "Yes."
Said I, "I have found something better."
"Better?"
"Yes."
"How?"

"Better for me, because I was always a poor hand at imitation. I imitated the minister with whom I settled from college, and nobody but myself and my wife ever guessed that my sermons were imitations of his. When I was a boy, my father had me taught drawing, and my master put before me something, and my copy needed to have letter-press underneath to state it was an imitation of the copy. And when I sat down to imitate Christ, no one could have guessed what I was trying to attain.

"But," said I, "my young friend, if my drawing-master could have infused the spirit of his skill into my brain and hand, he could have drawn through me as fair a drawing as his own; and if my great and noble friend could have only put his spirit into me, why should I not have spoken even as he? And if instead of imitating Christ far away in the glory, He will come by the Holy Ghost and dwell in me, by His grace He shall work through my poor yielded life, a life something like His own fair life." Christ liveth in me.

Many have no idea what religion is. Re-ligion, re-ligo, a Latin word meaning, "I bind,"—it is the binding of the heart to the Lord. No, I recall that; it is better: "He that is joined to the Lord is one spirit." O Christ, Thou art one with me, to make me one with Thee world without end!" [339]

Again, before you can *abide*, you must *attach*. Have you done that? Have you surrendered your heart and life to Jesus Christ? Have you invited and experienced his indwelling by the Holy Spirit? If not, read no further before you do. It can begin with a simple prayer (such as, "Be merciful to me, a sinner!"[340] or "Come into my heart, Lord Jesus; forgive my sin and take control"), but it will not end there. It may be a matter of renewing a commitment you made long ago. But attaching must precede abiding (though, to be accurate, your task is not to "join" yourself to the Lord, but to submit and invite him to do the "joining").

ATTUNE

If you have responded to the call of Jesus and surrendered your life to him, you have—at least in that moment and in that act—attuned your ears to his voice. You have heard him speak. You have responded to him. That act, that process, is one that must be continued if you hope to abide in him. Andrew Murray writes:

> As it was Jesus who drew you when He spake "Come," so it is Jesus who keeps you when He says "Abide." The grace to come and the grace to abide are alike from Him alone. That word come, heard, meditated on, accepted, was the cord of love that drew you nigh; that word abide is even so the band with which He holds you fast and binds you to Himself. Let the soul but take time to listen to the voice of Jesus. "In me," He says, "is thy place—in my almighty arms. It is I who love thee so, who speak Abide in me; surely thou canst trust me." The voice of Jesus entering and dwelling in the soul cannot but call for the response: "Yes, Saviour, in Thee I can, I will abide." [341]

How is this done?

Well, how did it start? How did you first hear the Lord's voice? Was it while reading the Bible? Was it a verse of scripture that drove home his call to your heart?

Was it the preaching of the Word? Was it a worship gathering? Was it the refrain of a hymn or the testimony of a saint? What was it?

It may have been a combination of such things, but the point is this: You heard his voice once. He used one or more means to pierce your heart with his love. He broke through to you as he did to Augustine, who writes in his *Confessions*:

You called, shouted, broke through my deafness;
you flared, blazed, banished my blindness;
you lavished your fragrance, I gasped, and now I pant for you;
I tasted you, and I hunger and thirst;
you touched me, and I burned for your peace. [342]

Whatever means God used before to break through your "deafness" and banish your "blindness," he may continue to use. Yet too often we drop such things as Bible reading and worshipping with others after we have "walked with Jesus" for a while, and so our attachment to him weakens and our attunement to his voice dulls.

One of the best ways to once more attune your spiritual ears to the voice of Jesus is the daily reading of his Word. You may read for days and weeks without any particular blessing or sense of his voice, but over time you will experience what Jesus meant when he spoke of his words abiding in you. [343] Your spirit will become more and more attuned to him, and his words will ring in your ears and come to rest in your mind and heart.

ATTEND

When you are like a shoot attached to the vine and your spirit is attuned to Jesus—especially by reading and hearing his Word—you have begun to abide in him. But you have not finished until you actively attend to him. Scot McKnight writes:

Sometimes it takes a jolt to get the point. And sometimes
Jesus is the one who has to provide the jolt, even to his closest
friends. Martha, a close friend of Jesus and his disciples,
needs a jolt, and Jesus gives it to her. In her own home, with
Jesus sitting in the "living room" teaching her sister, Mary,
Martha finds herself in the "kitchen" toiling away. Martha
is "distracted" with a Wall Street share of groaning and

grunting, and she lets Jesus know that Mary could poke her spoon into the pot to help. Jesus responds with wisdom drawn from deep wells:

> *Martha, Martha. . .you are worried and upset about many things, but only one thing is needed. Mary has chosen what is better, and it will not be taken away from her.*

What is that "one thing needed"? What distinguishes Martha's distraction from Mary's devotion? I suggest it is not so much their location as their posture.. . .

Mary's posture tells the story. Her posture is that of a student, of someone who wants to listen to what Jesus has to say, of someone who can wait for dinner. It is the posture, in fact, of someone who is so enthralled with Jesus that dinner might not even happen. . . .

At the feet of Jesus, Mary is seemingly serene. Mary's serenity derives from attending to Jesus, an expression that sums up Mary's posture. Humans, Jesus says, are defined not by their labor for him, as Martha thinks, but by their relationship to him, as Mary learns. [344]

What is *your* posture? Is it that of someone who hangs on Jesus' every word? Is it that of someone who can wait for dinner. . .or TV. . .or work? Is it that of someone who is so enthralled with Jesus that those things are secondary, at best?

You cannot experience joy, love, and all the fruit of the Spirit apart from Christ, and you cannot abide in Christ apart from prayer. Prayer as a priority. Prayer as passion. Prayer as one's portion. Andrew Murray writes:

> *How greatly the power to spend a day aright, to abide all the*

day in Jesus, depends on the morning hour. If the first-fruits be holy, the lump is holy. During the day there come hours of intense occupation in the rush of business or the throng of men, when only the Father's keeping can maintain the connection with Jesus unbroken. The morning manna fed all day; it is only when the believer in the morning secures his quiet time in secret to renew distinctly and effectually loving fellowship with his Saviour, that the abiding can be kept up all the day. But what cause for thanksgiving that it may be done! In the morning, with its freshness and quiet, the believer can look out upon the day. He can consider its duties and its temptations, and pass them through beforehand, as it were, with his Saviour, throwing all upon Him who has undertaken to be everything to him. Christ is his manna, his nourishment, his strength, his life: he can take the day's portion for the day, Christ as his for all the needs the day may bring, and go on in the assurance that the day will be one of blessing and of growth. . . . And so, each day separately, all the day continually, day by day successively, we abide in Jesus. [345]

When Jesus said, "Abide in me," he meant for you to be so connected to him—"each day separately, all the day continually, day by day successively"—that his Word to you and your words to him become your daily bread. Your manna. Your sustenance. And he promised that such abiding would result in love and joy, among other fruit.

THE FINAL WORD

That can be your experience. It really can. And it does not require a herculean effort. You can start small—by reading a psalm a day, perhaps, and praying for a few moments before leaving the house in the morning. As Brother Lawrence advises:

A little lifting up the heart suffices; a little remembrance of
God, one act of inward worship. . .[these] are prayers which,
however short, are nevertheless very acceptable to God. [346]

But do it now. Today, or tomorrow at the latest. Begin your
day, however busy it may promise to be, by praying for the grace
to begin. Continue asking for the grace to continue as you began.
Abide by asking for the grace to abide. *Each day separately, all the*
day continually, and day by day successively.

THE LAST WORD

An ordinary-looking man exits the freight elevator at Third Avenue Odd Lots and walks into an office. He greets the woman standing at a filing cabinet. "I'm looking for a special recording. Collector series."

"Well, I don't know. We have some record players and stuff—"

They are interrupted by a man in a tie and sweater vest. "I'll take care of the gentleman, Suzy. Would you get me last week's invoices, please?"

Suzy closes the file drawer and leaves the office. The man in the sweater vest closes the office door.

"Exactly what recording were you looking for?"

"Ivan in G, by Ernest Vaughn of the Ban Symphonic Orchestra, 1963."

Without a word, the man in the sweater vest walks to the desk, opens a lower drawer, and pulls out a red LP case. He hands it to the stranger and motions to the small phonograph in the corner of the office. Then he leaves.

The man takes a vinyl LP record out of the case, removes a cellophane wrapper, and places the disc on the phonograph. He sits as music starts to play. Then he moves the tone arm to the middle of the disc. There is no music, but a man's voice.

"Good morning, Mr. Briggs," says the voice. "General Rio Dominguez, the dictator of Santa Costa, makes his headquarters in the Hotel Nacionale. We've learned that two nuclear warheads furnished to Santa Costa by an enemy power are contained in the hotel vault. Their use is imminent. Mr. Briggs, your mission, should you decide to accept it, would be to remove both nuclear devices from Santa Costa. As always, you have carte blanche as to method and personnel, but, of course, should you or any member of your IM Force be caught or killed, the Secretary will disavow any knowledge of your actions. As usual, this recording will decompose one minute after the breaking of the seal."

The man rises from his chair and turns off the phonograph. The tone arm moves back to its perch and a second later smoke rises from the surface of the self-destructing record.

Thus begins the pilot episode of *Mission: Impossible*, a television series that debuted in September 1966. That opening scene, and others like it depicting Briggs (and in later seasons, Jim Phelps, played by Peter Graves) receiving his instructions on a recording that then self-destructs, became a hallmark of the show. The original series aired from 1966 to 1973, returned for two seasons from 1988 to 1990, and later spawned a series of movies starring Tom Cruise.

The idea of receiving word of an exciting, dangerous mission from a distant source fascinated audiences. But it was nothing new. Not even as far back as 1966. It reaches back more than nineteen hundred years before that.

THE SEVENTEENTH WORD

Sixteen chapters ago, we began exploring seventeen words of Jesus that can—and will—change our lives, if we will let them.

The first of those words was "Come."

The others are varied. Some are comforting, some are challenging. Some are delightful, and some are demanding.

"Follow."

"Take."

"Forgive."

"Rejoice."

But not one of these words is complicated. It ain't rocket

science, as they say. In fact, it ain't even high school algebra. When you get right down to it, the words and ways of Jesus are pretty doggone simple. Not necessarily *easy*. But *simple*.

And the last word? It was spoken by Jesus in Matthew 28:16-20, in which the Gospel writer records the last scene of Jesus' days on earth, after he had been crucified, after he rose from the dead, and after he spent forty days appearing to various people:

> *Then the eleven disciples went to Galilee, to the mountain where Jesus had told them to go. When they saw him, they worshiped him; but some doubted. Then Jesus came to them and said, "All authority in heaven and on earth has been given to me. Therefore go and make disciples of all nations, baptizing them in the name of the Father and of the Son and of the Holy Spirit, and teaching them to obey everything I have commanded you. And surely I am with you always, to the very end of the age."* [347]

You saw it. You heard it. The last word is "Go." One word. Two letters. One syllable.

If you are one of his followers, Jesus says to you, "Go." He gives you a mission. He entrusts you with a task. He issues you an assignment.

If you have truly "come," then he says to you, "Go." If you have heard and repented, he says to you, "Go." If you "follow," if you would "take," then you must "go."

If you "come" but don't "go," then whatever else you may be, you're not a follower of Jesus. . .because he says both to you. He intends for your going to be the outcome of your coming. And when Jesus says that one word, he packs a universe of meaning into those two tiny letters.

ACCEPT YOUR ASSIGNED MISSION

Hear Jesus' last words on earth as a *Mission: Impossible* assignment: "Your mission, should you choose to accept it, is to go and make disciples of all nations, baptizing them in the name of the Father and of the Son and of the Holy Spirit, and teaching them to obey everything I have commanded you."

"Go," Jesus said, "and make disciples."

Fair enough. But that prompts the question: Disciples of what? Followers of whom?

Followers of ourselves? Disciples of this church or that church? Of a particular denomination? Or ministry? Of some preferred theological viewpoint? Of certain cultural practices?

Of course not. When Jesus says, "Go and make disciples," he means for us to make more Jesus-followers. More men and women who sign up to follow *him* in *his* mission. But. . .

What is his mission?

Believe it or not, Jesus published his own mission statement. He spoke it originally through the prophet Isaiah, and then when he launched his earthly ministry from a village synagogue in his hometown, he announced it as his mission.

Luke the historian writes:

He came to Nazareth, where he had been brought up. And as was his custom, he went to the synagogue on the Sabbath day, and he stood up to read. And the scroll of the prophet Isaiah was given to him. He unrolled the scroll and found the place where it was written,

   "The Spirit of the Lord is upon me,
because he has anointed me
to proclaim good news to the poor.
He has sent me to proclaim liberty to the captives

and recovering of sight to the blind,
to set at liberty those who are oppressed,
to proclaim the year of the Lord's favor."

And he rolled up the scroll and gave it back to the attendant
and sat down. And the eyes of all in the synagogue were fixed
on him. And he began to say to them, "Today this Scripture has
been fulfilled in your hearing." [348]

In that moment, which Luke shows us followed immediately upon Jesus' baptism and temptation in the wilderness, Jesus provided his "mission statement" as the Messiah to the hometown crowd, in the synagogue he grew up in. He stated, matter-of-factly, "This is why I am here. This is my mission."

And it would have been understood, by everyone listening, that when Jesus sat down and began his teaching (which was how rabbis taught), he was applying to himself words that prophesied the Messiah, and that those words referred to the year of Jubilee.

You see, the Jews had a custom, ordained by God, not only that every seventh day of the week would be a Sabbath, a day of rest, but that every seventh year would also be a Sabbath, when the land itself would be given a rest from cultivation and productivity. And after every seventh Sabbath year (that is, every fiftieth year), there would be what was called the "year of Jubilee."

In that year, all slaves were to be set free, all men whose poverty had forced them to sell their lands would receive them back again, and those who had lost family members into slavery or imprisonment would be reunited with their loved ones.

So you can see why it was called the "Jubilee." And that is what Jesus said his mission was. What the law prescribed, what Isaiah had promised, Jesus said he fulfilled! He came to bring good news to the poor, the kind of news that was supposed to cause dancing in the streets every fifty years. He came to bring broken families together, to bind up the brokenhearted, to heal the hurting. He came to free the slaves, open the doors of darkness, untie men's hands, and unfold their wings. He came to proclaim the acceptable year, the year of God's grace, the year of Jubilee—but not once every fifty years; that was already supposed to be the case. Jesus came to bring a worldwide Jubilee that every year, every day, would speak good news to the poor, liberty to the captives, healing to the brokenhearted, forgiveness for the guilty, freedom for those who feel controlled, release for those who feel trapped, deliverance, laughter, relief, joy, Jubilee.

That was his mission.

And if that was *his* mission, it should be obvious that his followers or students or disciples would carry on his work. Right?

That is what we see happening in the Gospels, as Luke reports:

> *One day Jesus called together his twelve disciples and gave them power and authority to cast out all demons and to heal all diseases. Then he sent them out to tell everyone about the Kingdom of God and to heal the sick. "Take nothing for your journey," he instructed them. "Don't take a walking stick, a traveler's bag, food, money, or even a change of clothes. Wherever you go, stay in the same house until you leave town. And if a town refuses to welcome you, shake its dust from your feet as you leave to show that you have abandoned those people to their fate."*
>
> *So they began their circuit of the villages, preaching the Good News and healing the sick.* [349]

In the next chapter of Luke, Jesus sends off seventy more trained Jubilee-bringers with virtually the same instructions. That is, they were to heal and help and bless and bring good news. So when Jesus issues a final word—"Go and make disciples of all nations"—he is simply telling his disciples to carry on his mission of good news and freedom and healing to all nations (only now in light of his crucifixion, resurrection, and ascension).

The mission hasn't changed. What Jesus wants today is the same thing he has wanted all along—namely, people who are willing to spread the good news all over the place, setting captives free and binding up broken hearts.

Too often, however, even if we acknowledge intellectually that Jesus' mission was to "bring good news to the poor, proclaim freedom for the prisoner, recovery of sight for the blind, release the oppressed," we plan and program and function as if his mission was to create a comfy club for us to belong to, or a place to go five days a week so we don't have to rub elbows with people who don't already believe in Christ, or a cozy classroom where we can debate our heads off about what we believe, what others believe, and what everyone *ought* to believe.

Regardless of your career—truck driver, doctor, accountant, stockbroker, whatever—your mission in life, according to Jesus, is to spread his kingdom, to bring blessing to the poor, liberty to the captives, healing to the brokenhearted, forgiveness for the guilty, freedom for those who feel controlled, release for those who feel trapped, deliverance, laughter, relief, joy. . .Jubilee.

That is your mission, should you choose to accept it. Paul, the great church planter, said:

> *Life is worth nothing unless I use it for doing the work*
> *assigned me by the Lord Jesus—the work of telling others the*
> *Good News about God's mighty kindness and love.* [350]

That is the work assigned to you by the Lord Jesus. So accept it. That doesn't mean you have to go to seminary. It doesn't mean you have to become a preacher. It doesn't mean you have to stand on the corner of a busy city street screaming Bible verses into a bullhorn; in fact, I advise against it, because though that may fit your assigned mission to some extent, it does not fit your assigned method.

EMPLOY YOUR ASSIGNED METHOD

Paul writes, "Christ's love compels us."[351] Or, as Eugene Peterson paraphrases that verse in *The Message*: "Christ's love has moved [us] to such extremes. His love has the first and last word in everything we do."[352]

The first and last word in fulfilling our mission is to love people. It is to care about them. Bless them. Help them. Heal them.

When Jesus sent the Twelve—and then later the Seventy—out into the towns and villages all around, he equipped them and instructed them:

> *One day Jesus called together his twelve disciples and gave them power and authority to cast out all demons and to heal all diseases. Then he sent them out to tell everyone about the Kingdom of God and to heal the sick.* [353]

He specifically sent them out to *deliver* and *heal* while connecting what they were doing to the arrival of the kingdom of God. That is our mission, too. And notice how Jesus told them to react when things didn't go well:

> *"If a town refuses to welcome you, shake its dust from your feet as you leave to show that you have abandoned those people to their fate."* [354]

When we read that verse, it sounds a little vindictive, doesn't it? A little passive-aggressive, even. It has even entered our language as an idiom: "Shake the dust off your feet" means pretty much the same as "Good riddance to bad rubbish."

But there are other ways to understand that verse. First, Jesus' instructions would have made it clear that the disciples were not responsible for the response of other people to their mission of kindness. Jesus did not prescribe a codependent attitude, in which the disciples could be depressed or even destroyed by the rejection of others. He made it clear that those who were commissioned to "go" were answerable for *going*, not for others' *coming*.

Also, the instruction to shake the dust from their feet to make it clear that the hearers, not the bringers of the good news, were responsible can be seen as an act of respect, not hatred. Jesus' followers were not told to endlessly harangue or argue with people who were not receptive to their message; they were to move on in such a way that those who wouldn't listen might still be pricked in their conscience, even as the messengers left. Myron S. Augsburger writes:

> *There are implications here for modern mission. If we mean to serve others, we must serve others as they need to be served and not as we predetermine to serve them, for the latter is not service but dominance. The important thing. . .[is] making faith a possibility for people. In doing so we respect their freedom while making them aware of their responsibility. The blessing of grace depends upon the receptivity of the hearer.* [355]

God uses many ways to bring people into his kingdom. There have no doubt been some people who have been scared into the kingdom of God. There might also be some who could be nagged into the kingdom. But some ways are more effective than others. And neither of those methods has been specifically assigned to you. But love has.

Your method is love. Jude writes:

Show mercy to those whose faith is wavering. [356]

Go after those who take the wrong way. [357]

Have mercy on everyone who needs it. [358]

Reach out in mercy, grace, and love to all who need it. (And, at the risk of stating the obvious, *everyone* needs it.) Find ways to surprise people with love. Don't worry so much about correcting their wrong actions or bad language. Instead, help the captives find release, help the blind to see, help the oppressed to be set free, and help everyone experience the reality that the time of the Lord's favor has come. . .to them.

IMPROVISE THE APPROPRIATE MEANS

If your mission is to *go*, and your method is to *love*, what are the means by which you are to accomplish and fulfill your mission? How should you be going about this task Jesus has given you?

Obviously, first and foremost, you need to *live it*. The Bible says:

Show that [you] can be fully trusted, so that in every way [you] will make the teaching about God our Savior attractive. [359]

If you are a Christ-follower, God calls you to live in such a way that draws people to Jesus Christ, that attracts others to the kingdom of God. Is your life attracting anybody to Jesus? Is anybody interested in becoming a Christ-follower because of you? If not, ask yourself why. And when you answer, be honest with yourself. Your life is either smoothing people's path to Christ, or it is throwing obstacles in their way.

Beyond that, your means are as varied as you, your era, and your community. Remember what Jesus told the Twelve?

"Take nothing for your journey," he instructed them. "Don't take a walking stick, a traveler's bag, food, money, or even a change of clothes." [360]

And to the Seventy, he said:

"Don't take any money with you, nor a traveler's bag, nor an extra pair of sandals. And don't stop to greet anyone on the road." [361]

Interesting. One of the sent ones may well have been thinking, *Maybe I'll raise my staff like Moses did over the Red Sea and perform a mighty miracle.* Another may have remembered the boy's lunch of fish and loaves Jesus multiplied to feed thousands and thought, *I'd like to do something like that.* If they were thinking or planning anything like that, Jesus disabused them of such notions. He told them to go with just the shoes on their feet and the clothes on their back.

There may have been many good reasons for his instruction, but one reason might have been that their lack of natural resources would force them to depend on supernatural resources. Another might have been that they knew as they went that they would have to adapt. They would have to learn to "go with the flow." They might have to "wing it." Rather than imposing a certain agenda on this village or that town, they were free to respond both to the needs and to the resources of those they visited.

That place of dependence was probably the best place they could be. If Jesus had allowed them to take a supply of tracts with them, they would have handed out tracts, instead of sizing up and responding to the specific needs of the people. If they had been allowed to drive a bus across the landscape, they certainly would have started a bus ministry, whether or not the community really needed or wanted a bus ministry. If they had taken along supplies, they might have brewed tea, when everyone knows that coffee is a far better aid to the spread of the Gospel.

So how does all that apply to your mission? What would be the most effective means for use with your neighbors and friends? Is it a door-to-door survey? A tract? A "free prayer" booth at the county fair? An invitation to a church service? A platter of cookies? A seekers' small group? Something else?

It could be any of the above. Or none. Or all.

But because your assigned method is *love*, start there. Build a bridge by listening and caring. Someone told a story recently about a Chinese foreign exchange student some Christ-follower had helped to enter the kingdom of God. The exchange student, explaining how it happened, said, "That man cared for me. He built a bridge between my heart and his, and Jesus Christ walked across."

Everybody is hurting somewhere. The key to being effective in sharing the Good News is to listen. Eventually, one of those hurts or needs or interests is going to surface. When it does, you can do as those first disciples did and meet a need while relating what you're doing to the arrival of the kingdom of God.

USE THE PROPER MEASUREMENT

Once you respond to the last word from Jesus and embrace your assigned mission, employ your assigned method, and improvise the appropriate means, you can expect results. But you must use the proper measurement, or you are much more likely to excuse yourself, condemn yourself, or doubt God—none of which is helpful to you or glorifying to God.

No less godly a messenger than John the Baptist apparently used the wrong measurement in trying to assess his ministry, and even that of Jesus. After all, he'd not only been there at the beginning of Jesus' public ministry; he had announced it. It was John who shined the spotlight on Jesus of Nazareth and confidently proclaimed him as the Lamb of God to all who would hear. Perhaps more than anyone else, John believed that Jesus would usher in the kingdom of God. But when John was arrested and imprisoned, he thought surely something had gone wrong. He couldn't imagine a scenario in which the Messiah would allow his forerunner to suffer imprisonment and perhaps even death. Those things didn't jibe with John's expectations.

So John sent messengers to Jesus from his prison cell:

John, calling two of his disciples to him, sent them to the Lord, saying, "Are you the one who is to come, or shall we look for another?" And when the men had come to him, they said, "John the Baptist has sent us to you, saying, 'Are you the one who is to come, or shall we look for another?' " In that hour he healed many people of diseases and plagues and evil spirits, and on many who were blind he bestowed sight. And he answered them, "Go and tell John what you have seen and heard: the blind receive their sight, the lame walk, lepers are cleansed, and the deaf hear, the dead are raised up, the poor have good news preached to them." [362]

The results John suffered from *his* ministry caused him to question the authenticity of *Jesus'* ministry. But notice how Jesus answered John: he referred to his mission statement, the one he had issued in the synagogue at Nazareth. Of course, we don't know if John was present when Jesus read from Isaiah—though it is possible, as the two men were cousins. But there is no good reason to believe that John was there. When John asked, "Are You the Expected One, or do we look for someone else?"[363] Jesus answered, in effect, "Well, John, do you see me fulfilling the mission of the Messiah or not? Measure me by this: 'The blind receive their sight, the lame walk, lepers are cleansed, and the deaf hear, the dead are raised up, the poor have good news preached to them.' "[364]

If your mission is an extension of Jesus' mission, and if your method is love, that is the same measure you should use. Are people being helped and healed because you have brought the kingdom to them? Are people being comforted? Are they being loved? Are their lives more hopeful and joyful? Are you having a tangible effect on their lives? And do they know that to be a result of the rule and reign of Jesus Christ in your life?

That is the proper measurement. Changed lives. Because, as Jesus made clear to John, the measure of a mission is in its fulfillment, not in its good intentions.

THE FINAL WORD

There are no exemptions, no exceptions, to this final word. When Jesus says, "Go," he intends for every one of his followers around the world and throughout history to hear and obey. There are people in your world who need something that no one else can give them. They are waiting for someone that only you can be. You may not know who that person is. Then again, you may know *exactly* who that person is.

So the final word is this: *Go.*

Go to that person. In the margin next to this paragraph, write the name of at least one person to whom you can go. At least one person who needs to experience God's love through you. Below that name, list three practical ways you can meet that person's needs starting today (or tomorrow, at the latest). And then put this book in a place where it will remind you, in the coming days, to "go" to that person, in Jesus' name.

ENDNOTES

Chapter 1: The First Word

1. John 1:35–46 NIV.
2. John 1:38 NASB.
3. John 1:38 HCSB.
4. John 1:39 NIV.
5. Isaiah 1:18 KJV.
6. Psalm 34:8 ESV.
7. Malachi 3:10 ESV.
8. John 6:37 NIV.
9. Matthew 11:28–30 NIV.
10. Matthew 11:28 NIV.
11. Matthew 23:4 NLT.
12. Mark 3:3 ESV.
13. Mark 3:4 ESV.
14. Mark 8:23–25.
15. John 14:6.
16. Luke 14:28–32 GWT.
17. Luke 14:26–27, 33 GWT.
18. Dietrich Bonhoeffer, *The Cost of Discipleship* (New York: Touchstone, 1995), 89–90.
19. Hebrews 4:15 NIV (italics added).
20. Hebrews 2:18 NIV.
21. 1 Corinthians 10:13.
22. James 1:2–4 NIV

23. John 16:33 NIV.

24. Ibid.

25. Romans 8:37 ESV.

26. Luke 9:23 NLT.

27. Matthew 5:10–12 NIV.

28. 1 Peter 5:8 NIV.

29. 1 Peter 5:9 NIV.

30. 1 Peter 5:10 NIV.

31. Martin Luther, "A Mighty Fortress Is Our God," trans. Frederic Henry Hedge, public domain.

32. William True Sleeper, "Out of My Bondage, Sorrow, and Night," public domain.

Chapter 2: The Word for Starting Over

33. Luke 3:4–6 NIV.

34. Isaiah 40:10–11 NLT.

35. Matthew 4:17 ESV.

36. N. T. Wright, *The Challenge of Jesus* (Downers Grove, IL: InterVarsity, 1999), 43–44. Used by permission of InterVarsity Press, PO Box 1400, Downers Grove, IL 60515; www.ivpress.com.

37. Matthew 3:15 NIV.

38. Matthew 4:13–17 NIV.

39. Colossians 3:5 NLT.

40. Mark 1:14–15 NIV.

41. Eugene Peterson, *A Long Obedience in the Same Direction* (Downers Grove, IL: InterVarsity, 1980), 29–30.

42. Mark 1:15 NIV (italics added).

43. Scot McKnight, *The Jesus Creed* (Brewster, MA: Paraclete, 2004), 69. Used by permission of Paraclete Press. www.paracletepress.com.

44. Peterson, *Long Obedience*, 33.

45. Mark 1:15 NIV (italics added).

46. Luke 13:1–5 NLT.

47. John 3:7 NIV.

48. Peterson, *Long Obedience*, 30.

Chapter 3: The Word That Precedes Other Words

49. "About Us," GoodNewsNetwork, March 8, 2006; http://www.goodnewsnetwork.org/about-us.html.

50. Ibid.

51. Deuteronomy 6:4–9 NIV.

52. Deuteronomy 6:5 NIV.

53. Scot McKnight, *The Jesus Creed* (Brewster, MA: Paraclete, 2004), 7. Used by permission of Paraclete Press. www.paracletepress.com.

54. Matthew 22:36–40 NIV.

55. This phrase, "whoever has ears" (NIV), is recorded seven times in the Bible: Matthew 11:15; 13:9; 13:43; Mark 4:9; 4:23; Luke 8:8; 14:35.

56. Matthew 11:2–15 CEB.

57. Malachi 3:1; 4:5.

58. N. T. Wright, *The Challenge of Jesus* (Downers Grove, IL: InterVarsity, 1999), 38.

59. Luke 8:4–8 ESV.

60. Francis Chan, *Crazy Love: Overwhelmed by a Relentless God* (Colorado Springs: David C. Cook, 2013), 67. Copyright 2013 Francis Chan. Publisher permission required to reproduce. All rights reserved.

61. Genesis 35.

62. Matthew 13:24–30, 36–43 ESV.

63. Luke 8:12 NIV.

64. Matthew 13:26 ESV.

65. Matthew 13:29 ESV.

66. 2 Peter 3:9 ESV.

67. Mark 4:21–23 ESV.

68. Luke 14:34–35 ESV.

69. Ephesians 5:8 ESV.

Chapter 4: The Word That Invites

70. See Acts 2:42.

71. Matthew 9:9 NCV.

72. Ibid.

73. Ibid.

74. Mark 10:17–27 ESV.

75. See John 21:3.

76. Mark 10:20 ESV.

77. Deuteronomy 6:5 ESV.

78. Mark 10:22 ESV.

79. Luke 9:58 ESV.

80. Luke 9:61 NLT.

81. John 1:35–39 NIV.

82. Rob Bell, *Velvet Elvis: Repainting the Christian Faith* (Grand Rapids: Zondervan, 2005), 129–30.

83. Dallas Willard, *The Divine Conspiracy* (New York: HarperOne, 1998), 282. Reprinted by permission of HarperCollins Publishers.

84. Ibid., 282–83.

85. John 14:12 NIV.

86. Matthew 17:20 NIV.

Chapter 5: The Word That Satisfies

87. Henri Nouwen, *Life of the Beloved* (New York: Crossroad, 1994), 27. Used by permission.

88. Matthew 26:20–21, 26–29 NIV.

89. Luke 22:19 NLT.

90. Brennan Manning, *The Ragamuffin Gospel* (Sisters, OR: Multnomah, 2005), 59.

91. Luke 24:13–35 NIV.

92. See John 19:25.

93. Luke 24:30 NIV.

94. E. Earle Ellis, *New Century Bible: The Gospel of Luke* (London: Marshall, Morgan and Scott, 1974), 276.

95. John 21:12–19 NIV.

96. John 21:13 NIV.

97. Phillips Brooks, *The Candle of the Lord and Other Sermons* (Whitefish, MT: Kessinger, 2004), 246.

Chapter 6: The Word of Expectation

98. See John 8:58.

99. James 2:19 NIV.

100. Romans 4:3 NIV.

101. John 3:16 NIV.

102. See Matthew 9:18–31; Mark 5:22–43; and Luke 8:41–56.

103. See Luke 8:41–56.

104. Luke 8:22–25 NIV.

105. The Greek word for "leprosy" was used for a variety of chronic skin diseases, all of which made a person "unclean" and resulted in his or her banishment from human society.

106. William Barclay, *The Daily Bible Study Series: The Gospel of Mark*, rev. and updated ed. (Philadelphia: Westminster, [1975], 2001), 43.

107. Luke 5:12–14 ESV.

108. John 6:37 GWT.

109. Matthew 28:20 GNT.

110. John 14:3 ESV.

111. John 8:12 ESV.

112. John 8:23–24 ESV.

113. John 8:28 ESV.

114. John 8:56–59 NLT.

115. John 8:30 NLT.

116. John 6:35, 48, 51.

117. John 8:12.

118. John 10:7, 9.

119. John 10:11, 14.

120. John 11:25.

121. John 14:6.

122. John 15:1, 5.

123. Matthew 18:22 NIV.

124. 1 John 4:8.

125. Matthew 6:25 NIV.

126. Luke 6:38 NIV.

127. Mark 9:24 ESV.

Chapter 7: The Word That Opens Heaven

128. Luke 11:1 NIV.

129. Matthew 6:9–13 CJB.

130. Matthew 6:5–6 ESV.

131. Luke 11:2 ESV.

132. Romans 8:15 NLT.

133. Galatians 4:6 NLT.

134. Isaiah 6:1 NIV.

135. 1 Kings 22:19 NIV.

136. Revelation 4:3 MSG.

137. Isaiah 55:8–9 NLT.

138. Annie J. Flynt, "He Giveth More Grace," public domain.

139. Ephesians 3:20 GWT.

140. Dallas Willard, *The Divine Conspiracy* (New York: HarperOne, 1998), 258. Reprinted by permission of HarperCollins Publishers.

141. Matthew 6:10 NLT.

142. Willard, *Divine Conspiracy*, 260.

143. Luke 22:42 ESV.

144. Matthew 6:11 CEB.

145. Samuel Logan Brengle, *The Soul-Winner's Secret* (London: Salvationist, 1903), 12.

146. George Müller, *The Autobiography of George Müller* (New Kensington, PA: Whitaker House, 1985), 92.

147. Joseph M. Scriven, "What a Friend We Have in Jesus," public domain.

148. Psalm 51:17 NIV.

149. Matthew 6:12 CJB.

150. Luke 18:13 ESV.

151. Willard, *Divine Conspiracy*, 264–65. Reprinted by permission of HarperCollins Publishers.

152. Matthew 6:12 CJB.

153. Andrew Murray, *With Christ in the School of Prayer* (New Kensington, PA: Whitaker House, 1981), 106–8 (italics added).

154. W. Phillip Keller, *A Layman Looks at the Lord's Prayer* (Chicago: Moody, 1976), 120. Used with permission.

155. Matthew 6:12 CEB.

156. "Savior, Like a Shepherd Lead Us," attr. to Dorothy A. Thrupp. Public domain.

157. Matthew 6:13 ESV.

158. James 1:13 NLT.

159. Keller, *Lord's Prayer*, 137–38.

160. A shorter version appears in the *Didache*, 8:2, which scholars date to the late first century or early second century.

161. Matthew 6:13 CJB.

162. Matthew 6:9–13 HCSB.

Chapter 8: The Word That Frees

163. Luke 11:4 NLT.

164. Matthew 6:14 NLT.

165. Mark 11:25 ESV.

166. Luke 6:37 ESV.

167. Luke 23:34 ESV.

168. Scot McKnight, *The Jesus Creed* (Brewster, MA: Paraclete, 2004), 225. Used by permission of Paraclete Press. www.paracletepress.com.

169. Ibid.

170. Harper Lee, *To Kill a Mockingbird* (New York: HarperCollins, 1960; renewed © 1988 by Harper Lee; foreword copyright © 1993 by Harper Lee), 48. Reprinted by permission of HarperCollins Publishers.

171. Acts 7:54–60 NLT.

172. Matthew 5:44–45 MSG.

173. McKnight, *Jesus Creed*, 218.

174. Luke 23:34 ESV.

175. McKnight, *Jesus Creed*, 222.

176. Micah 7:19, Isaiah 43:25.

177. Jeremiah 50:20.

178. McKnight, *Jesus Creed*, 224–25 (italics in original).

179. 2 Corinthians 5:18–19 NIV.

180. McKnight, *Jesus Creed*, 226.

181. Romans 12:18 NLT.

182. Luke 23:34 ESV.

183. Luke 23:46 NIV.

184. Frederica Matthewes-Green, "Forgiveness Vespers," March 20, 2000; http://www.frederica.com/writings/forgiveness-vespers.html. Used with permission.

Chapter 9: The Word on Which All Words Hang

185. Oscar Hammerstein II and Jerome Kern, "Can't Help Lovin' Dat Man," copyright © 1927 T. B. Harms & Company, Inc., Universal Music Publishing Limited.

186. Matthew 22:37–40 NIV.

187. E. Stanley Jones, *Abundant Living* (New York: Abingdon-Cokesbury, 1942), 133.

188. Romans 13:10 NIV.

189. Matthew 22:34–40 NIV.

190. Deuteronomy 6:4–5 NIV.

191. https://www.savannahbee.com/product/Tupelo-Honey/ST-302

192. BOGOF = Buy One Get One Free.

193. Leviticus 19:18 NIV.

194. Luke 10:25 NIV.

195. Luke 10:26–27 NIV.

196. Luke 10:28–37 NIV.

197. Wendell Berry, *Blessed Are the Peacemakers: Christ's Teachings about Love, Compassion and Forgiveness* (Berkeley, CA: Shoemaker & Hoard, 2005), 62.

198. Matthew 22:37, 39 NIV (italics added).

199. See Ephesians 5:29 ESV.

200. Luke 7:39 ESV.

201. Luke 7:40–47 ESV.

202. Dallas Willard, *The Divine Conspiracy* (New York: HarperOne, 1998), 183. Reprinted by permission of HarperCollins Publishers.

Chapter 10: The Word That Sings and Dances

203. Quentin Hardy, "Global Slavery, by the Numbers," *Bits*, March 6, 2013; http://bits.blogs.nytimes.com/2013/03/06/global-slavery-by-the-numbers/?_r=0.

204. Tony Dokoupil, "The Suicide Epidemic," *Newsweek*, May 22, 2013.

205. John 16:33 CEV.

206. Isaiah 53:3 NLT.

207. John 1:10 NLT.

208. John 1:11 MSG.

209. Dallas Willard, *The Divine Conspiracy* (New York: HarperOne, 1998), 64. Reprinted by permission of HarperCollins Publishers.

210. Matthew 11:19.

211. Matthew 17:4.

212. Psalm 16:11 ESV.

213. Henri J. M. Nouwen, *Here and Now: Living in the Spirit* (New York: Crossroad, 1994), 29. Used by permission.

214. John Calvin, quoted in Thomas F. Tierney, *The Value of Convenience: Genealogy of Technical Culture* (Albany, NY: SUNY, 1992), 128.

215. Ann Voskamp, *Selections from One Thousand Gifts: Finding Joy in What Really Matters* (Grand Rapids: Zondervan, 2012), 6 (italics in original).

216. Charles Haddon Spurgeon, *The Treasury of David* (Grand Rapids: Kregel, 1976), 161.

217. Luke 1:47 NLT.

218. Luke 10:17 NLT.

219. Luke 10:20 NLT.

220. Romans 15:7.

221. Ephesians 1:7 NIV.

222. Samuel Logan Brengle, *Take Time to Be Holy: 365 Daily Inspirations to Bring You Closer to God*, ed. Bob Hostetler (Carol Stream, IL: Tyndale Momentum, 2013), 318.

223. John 4:35–36 NASB.

224. Luke 19:37–38 NIV.

225. John 20:19–20 NASB.

226. Luke 22:15 MSG.

227. Matthew 5:11–12 ESV.

228. James 1:2–4 NLT.

229. Elisabeth Kübler-Ross, *Death: The Final Stage of Growth* (New York: Simon and Schuster, 1975), 96.

230. Matthew 5:12 ESV.

231. Robert Browning, "Rabbi Ben Ezra," *Poems of Robert Browning* (London: Oxford University, 1923), 636.

232. Romans 8:18 PHILLIPS.

233. Luke 10:41 ESV.

234. Andrew Murray, *Abide in Christ* (Fort Washington, PA: Christian Literature Crusade, 1968), 143 (italics added).

235. Leonard Sweet, *Soul Salsa: 17 Surprising Steps for Godly Living in the 21st Century* (Grand Rapids: Zondervan, 2000), 189.

236. Philippians 4:4 NIV.

Chapter 11: The Word for a Dark World

237. Matthew 5:14–16 NIV.

238. Matthew 5:14 NIV.

239. Matthew 5:14 ESV.

240. Matthew 5:10–12 ESV.

241. Matthew 5:16 ESV.

242. Matthew 5:14; John 8:12.

243. Matthew 5:16 MSG.

244. Randy Harris, *Living Jesus: Doing What Jesus Says in the Sermon on the Mount* (Abilene, TX: Leafwood, 2012), 38. Used by permission of Leafwood Publishers, an imprint of Abilene Christian University Press.

245. Ibid., 40.

246. Matthew 5:16 NIV.

247. Matthew 6:1 PHILLIPS.

248. John Gill, "Commentary on Matthew 5:16," in *The New John Gill's Exposition of the Entire Bible*; http://www.biblestudytools.com/commentaries/gills-exposition-of-the-bible/matthew-5-16.html.

249. Acts 10:38 ESV.

250. Guy Malone, "A 'Tip' for Christians Who Dine Out"; http://www.guymalone.com/tipping.htm. Used with permission.

251. Matthew 5:16 NIV.

252. 1 Peter 2:12 NIV.

253. Colossians 4:5 NIV.

254. 2 Corinthians 9:11 NIV.

255. Luke 7:35 NLT.

256. Matthew 5:16 ESV.

Chapter 12: The Word of Warning

257. Matthew 10:16–23 ESV.

258. John 2:23–25 NLT.

259. Mark 8:11–15 NLT.

260. Mark 12:38–40 NLT.

261. Luke 12:1–3 NLT.

262. Larry Osborne, *Accidental Pharisees: Avoiding Pride, Exclusivity, and the Other Dangers of Overzealous Faith* (Grand Rapids: Zondervan, 2012), 37.

263. See Mark 7:10–12.

264. See Matthew 23:27.

265. Matthew 6:1–8 NIV.

266. Osborne, *Accidental Pharisees*, 45–46.

267. Philippians 2:3–4 MSG.

268. Luke 12:13–15 NASB.

269. See Luke 10:41–42.

270. Luke 12:15 NLT.

271. Matthew 7:15–20 NLT.

272. William Barclay, *The Daily Bible Study Series: The Gospel of Matthew*, vol. 1 (Philadelphia: Westminster Press, 1975), 282–83.

273. Matthew 7:16 NLT.

Chapter 13: The Word of Abundance

274. Andrew Murray, *Abide in Christ* (Fort Washington, PA: Christian Literature Crusade, 1968), 93.

275. Matthew 6:2–3; Luke 12:33 ESV.

276. Matthew 10:8 ESV.

277. Matthew 19:21; Mark 10:21 ESV.

278. Luke 6:30 ESV.

279. Luke 6:38 ESV.

280. Matthew 10:8 NLT.

281. Matthew 6:2 ESV (italics added).

282. Luke 14:12 ESV (italics added).

283. Luke 14:13 ESV (italics added).

284. Acts 20:35 GNT.

285. Henri Nouwen, *Life of the Beloved: Spiritual Living in a Secular World* (New York: Crossroad, 1992), 85. Used by permission.

286. Luke 2:1–7 NIV.

287. Luke 2:7 NIV.

288. Romans 12:13 NIV.

289. 1 Peter 4:9 MSG.

290. See 1 Timothy 3:2; Titus 1:8; and 1 Timothy 5:10.

291. Luke 2:16 NIV.

292. Robert Wicks, *Availability: The Spiritual Joy of Helping Others* (New York: Crossroad, 1986), 1–2.

293. Matthew 2:1–2 PHILLIPS.

294. Matthew 9–12 PHILLIPS.

295. Matthew 10:8 NLV.

296. Matthew 10:8 HCSB.

297. Luke 6:30 ESV.

298. Matthew 10:8 NLT.

299. See Matthew 6:2–4.

300. Luke 21:1–4.

301. E. Stanley Jones, *Abundant Living* (New York: Abingdon-Cokesbury, 1942), 218.

302. Leonard Sweet, *Soul Salsa: 17 Surprising Steps for Godly Living in the 21st Century* (Grand Rapids: Zondervan, 2000), 56.

303. Job 2:11–13 NIV.

304. Matthew 10:8 NLT.

Chapter 14: The Word of Inclusion

305. Kipling D. Williams, "The Pain of Exclusion," *Scientific American*, January/February 2011, 30–37.

306. See Matthew 4:18–19.

307. John 1:35–42 NIV.

308. John 6:7–9 NIV.

309. John 12:20–22 NIV.

310. See John 1:43–51.

311. Matthew 19:13–15 MSG.

312. John 4:7–9 NIV.

313. "About Servant Evangelism"; http://www.servantevangelism.com/about-servant-evangelism.

314. Luke 14:7–11 NIV.

315. Mark 10:45 MSG.

316. Matthew 14:17 ESV.

317. Matthew 14:18 ESV.

318. Matthew 17:17 ESV.

319. Luke 14:12–14 NIV.

320. Matthew 9:10–11 NIV.

321. Matthew 11:19 NIV.

322. Richard Rohr, *Yes, and . . .: Daily Meditations* (Cincinnati: Franciscan Media, 2013), 200.

Chapter 15: The Word That Stoops

323. John 13:13–15 NIV.

324. Matthew 20:25–28 NIV.

325. Mark 9:35 NIV.

326. Matthew 23:11 NIV.

327. William Booth, quoted in John R. W. Stott, *The Incomparable Christ* (Downers Grove, IL: InterVarsity, 2001), 155.

328. Samuel Logan Brengle, *Take Time to Be Holy: 365 Daily Inspirations to Bring You Closer to God*, Bob Hostetler, ed. (Carol Stream, IL: Tyndale Momentum, 2013), 133.

329. John 13:15 NIV (italics added).

330. 1 Peter 5:5 GNT.

331. John 13:12 NIV.

332. Matthew 25:40 NIV.

333. Matthew 25:45 NIV.

Chapter 16: The Word That Clings

334. John 15:1–11 ESV.

335. John 15:5 ESV.

336. Luke 18:13 ESV.

337. See Ezekiel 36:26.

338. See 2 Corinthians 5:17.

339. F. B. Meyer, *Christ-Life for Your Life* (Chicago: Moody, 1983), 49–50. Used with permission.

340. Luke 18:13 ESV.

341. Andrew Murray, *Abide in Christ* (Fort Washington, PA: Christian Literature Crusade, 1968), 23.

342. Augustine, *The Confessions*, trans. Marie Boulding (New York: New City, 1997), 262.

343. See John 15:7.

344. Scot McKnight, *The Jesus Creed* (Brewster, MA: Paraclete, 2004), 192–93 (italics in original). Used by permission of Paraclete Press. www.paracletepress.com.

345. Murray, *Abide in Christ*, 85–86.

346. Brother Lawrence, *The Practice of the Presence of God* (London: Epworth, 1963), 34.

Chapter 17: The Last Word

347. Matthew 28:16–20 NIV.

348. Luke 4:16–21 ESV.

349. Luke 9:1–6 NLT.

350. Acts 20:24 TLB.

351. 2 Corinthians 5:14 NIV.

352. 2 Corinthians 5:14 MSG.

353. Luke 9:1–2 NLT.

354. Luke 9:5 NLT.

355. Myron S. Augsburger, *The Communicator's Commentary: Matthew*, vol. 1 (Waco, TX: Word, 1982), 135.

356. Jude 22 NLT.

357. Jude 1:23 MSG.

358. Jude 1:23 CEV.

359. Titus 2:10 NIV.

360. Luke 9:3 NLT.

361. Luke 10:4 NLT.

362. Luke 7:18–22 ESV.

363. Luke 7:20 NASB.

364. Luke 7:22 ESV.

NOTES

NOTES

NOTES

NOTES

NOTES

NOTES